Praise for this

"This publication is timely. As the business of making a living from music gets harder this is an essential guide to ways of getting help, and learning the language needed to get that help. There's probably no such thing as easy money from any funder, but as a funder who cares about true talent finding its way, anything that makes it more likely that talent and funding find each other is very welcome. Remi Harris provides a clear and much needed guide to navigating the tricky geography of the funding landscape."

Alan Davey, CEO, Arts Council England

"We live in interesting times; the long term assignment of rights in return for investment is no longer the only option available for musicians and songwriters. The MU has long advocated the DIY approach for progressing a career as a musician and this much-needed guide to raising the necessary funds is a timely and invaluable tool in achieving independence and success."

Horace Trubridge, General Secretary, Musicians' Union

"Artists and small music companies have more control than ever, but navigating the world of funding and finance is a daunting task. The attention to detail, pertinent case studies and practical advice in Remi Harris' comprehensive guide make this essential reading for the DIY sector."

Joe Frankland, CEO, PRS Foundation

"Being an independent artist today inevitably also means being an entrepreneur. In order to thrive and create a sustainable career, I believe a tangible understanding of funding is essential. Remi is an expert in her field of funding and music business consultancy. She sincerely cares about the artists she works with, pushing for their continued success and shining a bright light in an often dark landscape of funding that can feel quite complex and intimidating. Remi is an industry treasure and this book is golden."

Ayanna Witter-Johnson, Independent Artist / Hill and Gully Records

"Investment in British creative talent is at a critical juncture. As our nation struggles to move investment focus away from industrial concerns to internet-driven, knowledge-based youth enterprise, this publication is significant in both its timing and content. British music is a leading light in the creative field, a rare export jewel. Investment in music talent will define whether this sector will grow or decline; it's as simple as that. Easy Money? A Definitive UK Guide to Funding Music Projects will prove a useful tool in helping us push towards the hoped for outcome."

Brian Message, ATC Management and Chairman, MMF

EASY MONEY?

The Definitive UK Guide to Funding Music Projects

REMI HARRIS

REMI HARRIS
CONSULTING

Copyright © 2013 Remi Harris

The right of Remi Harris to be identified as the author of this work has been asserted in accordance with the UK Copyright, Designs and Patents Act 1988.

All rights reserved. No part of this publication may be reproduced, stored in a retrieval system, or transmitted in any form or by any means electronic mechanical, photocopying, recording or otherwise, except as permitted by the UK Copyright, Designs, and Patents Act 1988, without the prior written permission of Remi Harris.

First published 2013 by Music Tank Publishing Ltd, London.

This edition published 2020 by Remi Harris Consulting.

A catalogue record for this title is available from the British Library.

ISBN: 978-1-9160278-0-0 (Paperback Edition)

ISBN: 978-1-9160278-1-7 (Ebook Edition)

Cover design: Ebook Launch Team

Figure design: Tierna Byrne Marketing and Design

Contents

How to Use This Guide

You'll find Easy Money to be both a reference guide you can dip into to find out about a specific funding source and an ordered, comprehensive guide to the six key funding options available. The information within will make the process of getting funding for a music project in the UK easier and more accessible.

The chapters are ordered from the relatively straightforward to the complex based on the cost, time and complexity of getting the funding. The book begins with grants which should be low cost to no cost to access and usually have a clear, published process as to how applications are awarded. It then looks at money from friends and family, crowdfunding and sponsorship before considering commercial lending, whether that be debt or investment finance.

This guide contains several features to help you – detailed descriptions of funding sources; case studies of artists and music businesses who have won funding; an analysis of the application procedure; and insider tips and links to sources of funding and further information. The case studies themselves are intended to stand alone, for those preferring to learn from real-life examples, or may be read as a supplement to the main body of each chapter.

The chapters explain the basic principles of each funding type and also provide analyses of their relevance for music projects together with some of the history and policy relating to them. This context is often missing from guides that are promoting one particular type of funding or another.

A key purpose of this guide is to give you an 'unvarnished' perspective that will help those seeking music funding to better understand the motivations and requirements of their funder, and not present an unrealistically rosy picture of the procedure when it is actually quite hard work! Encouraging you to look beyond your own project to understand the funder on the other side of the equation is an important part of what I hope to achieve with Easy Money.

These chapters also contain a lot of factual information about how funding is arranged and are informed by interviews with some key organisations and funding advisers. I approached both the case studies and the interviews as if I were a musician or a music company looking for money, and asked all the questions I could about how to approach the funder and how to make applications successful.

Each of the main funding chapters concludes with links to additional information and sources of funding, with suggestions for further reading.

WHO IS THIS GUIDE FOR?

This guide is written for the individuals and small businesses which make up the overwhelming majority of 'the music industry', and I am imagining that the reader is someone who works for a record label, publisher, promoter or management company; is a performer; wants to run a music-related social business such as a festival; or is an individual musician or band member who wishes to get money to further their career. This guide is also written from the perspective of someone working within 'contemporary popular music' or 'commercial music' – the world that I know best. That is not to say that it will not be relevant for those involved in folk, jazz, chamber music or other genres.

The information included is pitched at entities smaller than a music multinational or major orchestra, whose size and structure make their funding requirements clearly distinct from those that make up the majority of the music industry, approximately 98 per cent of which comprises musicians, micro and small businesses and music projects that require funding[1],[2].

It will also be of interest to those acquainted with one particular area of funding who may wish to learn about other routes.

WHAT THIS BOOK WILL NOT DO

I want to make it clear that reading this book will not automatically lead to you securing funding. Some ideas, business models and performers are simply bad. Some are good, but don't have the right people running them. Some simply will not be presented in the right way to the right funders, or will be presented perfectly, just to the wrong funder.

If you do have a good idea, the information contained within will give you a realistic picture of the likelihood and routes to success for getting money. It will help you to identify the right source to target and will inform you about how best to present your idea.

I hope that this book will improve the quality of applications to funders and that as a result, they will be encouraged to put their money into music.

FUNDING AND FUNDERS: A DEFINITION

I have found that the terms 'funding', 'finance' and 'investment' tend to be used interchangeably. I have heard people talking about money borrowed from the bank or money received in the form of grants as 'investment', whereas I would define the term 'investment' as being money used to buy shares in a company or a stake in ownership in anticipation of a share of profits.

In this guide, I am using the word 'money' or sometimes 'funding' (or 'finance') to mean 'financial resources provided to make some project possible', whether the money comes from commercial organisations, private individuals or public sources. I use the term 'funders' to mean the people who provide the money, whether they are participants in a crowdfunding campaign, or a bank providing a loan. It is really important to make it clear that when I say 'funding' I do not mean only public money – which is what some people automatically associate with that term – but also commercial investment, corporate sponsorship and other sources of money described in this guide, as identified below.

ABOUT THIS REPRINT

This guide was originally published by Music Tank (University of Westminster) in 2013, and retains its original text and links. Where possible links have been checked and updated, where not possible the original links have been retained. Readers should note that some of the information, organisations, funds and statistics included have changed between 2013 and this reprint in 2020. However due to continuing demand for the guide and the large amount of general principles and themes it contains I have decided to issue it in its original format. End notes have been added to the text, wherever I was aware of a change of name for a fund or funder.

ONE

Introduction

Over the 11 years I spent at the Association of Independent Music (AIM), a UK music industry trade association representing the independent music sector, I unintentionally became known as its funding expert. This was partly because I had some success in raising money for the organisation by way of public grants and other income-generating initiatives.

As a result, when AIM received phone calls from an independent record label or musician wanting to know about 'funding', they would be put through to me. At AIM, we prided ourselves on giving out helpful advice on the spot, but after these funding calls, I always felt that I'd failed to do so satisfactorily – I just didn't have the right information available.

This guide is an attempt to provide a practical and detailed answer to the question asked by so many of those individuals: "How can I get funding for my music?"

Over the decade 2000–2010, there were sweeping changes to record companies, as highlighted by Tony Wadsworth in his 2011 MusicTank report Remake, Remodel: The Evolution of the Record Label[1]. As Wadsworth wrote, record companies remain the largest source of money for marketing and developing new music. However, both the number of projects that record companies can fund and the amount of alternative funding available, to small labels in particular, has contracted. This, in turn, has adversely affected publishers, performers, songwriters and managers.

In 2000, what I call the 'intra-industry funding model' was still dominant in the music business. This meant that most of the money sought by small firms and bands was provided by other companies in the music sector; an example being deals between physical distributors and small labels, whereby distributors provided a line of credit to labels, that were then able to fund the manufacture and promotion of their physical product.

At that time there was also a reasonable spread of larger independent and multinational companies that could be approached for deals in the live, recording and publishing sectors, many of which involved an offer of advance payments that facilitated the development of writers' and performers' careers. These companies were either profitable, allowing them to reinvest their profits into these deals, or were able to access investment and loans, making this model possible.

Even during that period, there was concern about the limited money available to invest in music, particularly in support of smaller companies and artists. This became a key part of the industry's lobbying agenda, and the issue became known as the 'access to finance' problem: it is one that this sector continues to raise with the UK Government.

The access to finance issue has been thoroughly researched, and some understanding of that research is necessary for anyone who wants to get the most from this guide. This is because many of the funding and taxation arrangements that affect the music sector are influenced by government policy.

A commonly held and longstanding view is that there is a funding gap for small businesses; some sort of disconnect between businesses worthy of funding and the potential funding on offer. This notion is often traced back to an important 1931 report that emerged from a government committee chaired by Harold Macmillan, with committee members including economist John Maynard Keynes and Lord Bevin. The committee had set out to investigate sources of funding to stimulate an economic revival following the Great Crash[2]. However in his 2008 book, Venture Capital Funding[3], author Stephen Bloomfield describes the perceived funding gap as a myth, deeming it:

> "A general belief amongst business people, officials and government ministers that it is impossible to get funding for a deal... unless it is worth many millions of pounds."

Historically, the music industry continued to argue that there was a funding gap for small businesses up until 1997, when the incoming New Labour Government appeared to have listened to its concerns. There was hope that the situation might improve, especially given the arrival of the newly established Department of Culture, Music and Sport (DCMS)[4].

One of the first significant pieces of research into music industry funding was Banking On A Hit: The Funding Dilemma For Britain's Music Businesses[5]. One of its 17 recommendations emphasised the importance of "improving the level of understanding between the music industry and financiers".

At the time, the CEO of AIM, Alison Wenham said:

> "The British music industry is undoubtedly one of Britain's most successful sectors and one of our greatest exports. Small and Medium Sized Enterprises (SME)[6] companies are the jewel in its crown, and many would do even better with an appropriate level of investment."

By 2006, the music industry had been thoroughly disrupted by digital technology, and, despite much lobbying, there was no solution in sight for the access to finance problem. There were complaints that the recommendations made in Banking on A Hit had not been implemented.

That same year, the DCMS commissioned the report SME Music Businesses: Business Growth and Access To Finance[7], a survey of music companies and musicians that revealed a serious lack of knowledge and preparedness with respect to finance among participants. The report stated:

> "There seems to be a gap between the music business SMEs' subjective ambitions and perceptions of the challenges they face and the objective business challenges that they face. If this gap persists, it seems likely that many of the music businesses will continue to struggle with the day-to-day running of their businesses, have low profitability and will not be able to achieve... commercial and arguably creative growth."

I was concerned about some of the findings of this research, in particular one conclusion that:

> "only 61 per cent [of music companies surveyed] believed budgets and forecasts were useful".

In fact, most of the respondents were musicians who were unlikely to have ever required business plans. Furthermore, some of the most profitable independent record companies, such as the Beggars Group, shared the view that forecasts were of limited use when it came to predicting record sales. In any case, the impact of the research was minimal: little was done following its completion, although the DCMS continued to publish its occasionally updated Music Money Map[8] – a listing of funders who in some way relate to music.

More recently, in 2010 and 2011, I conducted research for UK Music into retail bank lending and found that music companies were reporting very poor access to sources of finance. In fact, I could only locate one use of the Government's Enterprise Finance Guarantee (EFG)[9] scheme by a music company (that wished to remain anonymous). The research was presented as evidence to a House of Commons Select Committee[10], which criticised the scheme. In the same year, UK Music was also a co-funder of an independent report called Risky Business by the think tank Demos[11], which took the view that although there was no hard evidence that creative companies were riskier than companies in other sectors (measured by the rate of business closure by sector), bank loans were probably unsuitable for music companies because of the unpredictability of their type of creative product.

Also in 2011, the Creative Industries Council (CIC)[12] was formed in order to bring together the creative industries and government departments. One of the three key concerns on the table was, of course, access to finance.

Overall, the music industry has been successful in relaying the message about its need for funding and financial support to successive governments, but has found no success in securing any special policy changes; such as the investment tax breaks available to the film and more recently the computer games industries. Nor has it been able to get permission for other support such as eligibility for research and development tax credits for developing new music. While industry lobbying will doubtless continue, a number of government reports have challenged the music industry to be better informed about finance. This guide is an attempt to meet that challenge.

THE SIX SOURCES OF MONEY

I have identified six key sources of money that are the most relevant and appropriate for small music companies and musicians. Chapters three to eight are dedicated to each of them in turn, with case studies from successful applicants, interviews with funders, tips for applying to funders for money and a list of funders related to each source.

The six sources of money are grant-making bodies, friends and family, crowds and crowdfunding, sponsors, lenders and investors.

1. Grant-Making Bodies

They are, as previously stated, what most people think of when they hear the word 'funding'. There are those such as the PRS for Music Foundation[13], the various arts councils, the Musicians' Benevolent Fund[14] and EMI Sound Foundation that are specifically set up in order to offer grants for different sorts of music projects and musicians. There are also scores of other grant-making trusts and foundations (see Additional Trusts and Foundations). I will not offer a comprehensive list, but I will explain how they work, and when and where to apply.

2. Friends and Family

They're known as part of the 'three Fs' of 'Friends, Family and Fools' in investment texts. Studies of both the music industry, and small businesses in general, show that using one's own money or money borrowed from loved ones is the most common source of small business finance. It is important that music companies and projects know this and consider whether to, and/or how to use it. This book will consider how this source of finance might be structured.

3. Crowds and Crowdfunding

These have always been around; historically, many art works have been funded by public subscription. Online peer-to-peer platforms have made this far easier and are increasingly looked upon as being a viable way to fund music projects, whereby interaction with fans is an essential precursor to securing financial backing.

4. Sponsors

Sponsors are included because they are appealing to many small businesses and individuals who tend to feel more comfortable with direct commercial deals than with bank loans or grants. In addition, there have also been a number of high-profile music sponsorship deals that show that they can work well for both sides.

5. Lenders

This has been included due to the widespread concern expressed about the lack of readily available finance across the music sector, with 'finance' in this instance taken to mean debt. Debt means borrowing money from lenders, whether in the form of overdrafts, bank loans or other business credit and personal credit, such as mortgages and credit cards. Debts may also take the form of 'soft' loans provided by development agencies and others.

6. Investors

Investors are of key importance, because it is their money that government and researchers agree is the most suitable for 'risky' businesses, yet for many this is a misunderstood source of finance. Many music businesses feel investment is out of their reach and only available for people involved in multi-million pound deals. On the contrary, investment can be for any amount, as this guide will demonstrate.

THE FIVE FUNDING STAGES

While all of these sources of money differ from one another, I believe there are five key stages in the cycle of obtaining money that apply to all of these. A six-stage model is often used for grants and donations, but I think five works better for the purposes of this book.

These stages are idea developing, assessing, acquiring, delivering and reporting.

Of course, there is a certain amount of luck involved in the process, and it is not the case that every story of funding success neatly follows these stages. That said, these steps are a useful way to break down the process in order to analyse it. In many of the following chapters I discuss research, presentation, communication and reporting matters as they apply to working with each different type of funder.

1. Idea Developing

You must have a firm idea of what you want to do, which is either strong in a conventional way or original and distinctive. Avoid vagueness as it can be counter-productive.

2. Assessing

You must find a funder that is a strong fit with you and your idea. Approaching people with no interest in your type of project is a waste of time.

3. Acquiring

To acquire the money you must learn what the funder wants and how to speak their language, using this knowledge to modify your approach. Approaching funders without knowing anything about them is going to make you an unappealing funding proposition.

4. Delivering

While your project is 'live' you must be willing to build a relationship with the funder. There must be a two-way flow of benefit, and you must communicate in a clear and consistent way with them during the delivery of whatever it is that you have been given the money to do. Falling silent for several months after you have received the money is no way to build a mutually beneficial, lasting relationship.

5. Reporting

Finally, you must report back to close the project. The quality of your report to funders about what you have delivered may well play an important part in determining whether or not they are willing to work with you again in the future. Remember to ask yourself what the funder gets out of the interaction that would keep them interested in your future projects and ideas.

FUNDING SUCCESS RATES

It's difficult to estimate the rates of success of the different funding sources outlined in this book, as there are so many factors at play and a limited amount of transparency and data. However I have attempted to give an estimate from the information available. I was not able to access data on sponsorship and friends and family.

1. Grants

Success rates range between 10 and 33 per cent depending on the fund.

Eligibility is vital – a large proportion of applications rule themselves out of a chance of success simply by not meeting eligibility criteria! Unsurprisingly, the chances of gaining funding greatly increase by actually being eligible. Funds awarding a limited number of grants or which are high profile are usually the most competitive (and oversubscribed).

Interviews with funding experts reveal success rates typically ranging between ten and 33 per cent of all applications received, depending on the fund. ACE's Grants for the Arts programme similarly indicates that application success rates range between 30 to 40 per cent of all first- time applications received[15].

PRSF's general funds reach approximately 16 per cent of all applications; the British Music Abroad Scheme funds ten per cent of all applications; the very high demand for Momentum Music (round one) resulted in just ten out of 500 applications being successful – a success rate of roughly two per cent[16].

Trusts and foundations generally have a 33 per cent success rate according to the Directory of Social Change; typically one third of applications are ineligible (with the remaining third being unsuccessful)[17].

2. Crowdfunding

Between 43 and 76 per cent of projects draw down money at the end of a crowdfunding campaign.

This form of funding is most under your control, so success rates can be relatively high – but many projects won't have enough potential supporters, or enough work put into them to reach their goals. Plan well and put in the work needed and you will maximise your chances of success.

Success depends on the readiness of the project and level of effort put in. Kickstarter claims 43 per cent of all campaigns achieve their funding target and that 52 per cent of all music projects similarly achieve their target[18].

When interviewed, Pledge Music stated that their success rate was "about 76 per cent of all campaigns"[19].

Crowdfunding sites with an all-or-nothing policy do not allow the drawdown of funds unless the fundraising target is reached, meaning their success rates will be lower than those for platforms that allow part-funded campaigns to take receipt of funds.

3. Debt Finance

Approval rates range between 43 and 80 per cent for all SMEs (not just within the music sector).

These figures include sizeable SMEs - businesses with up to 250 staff. Micro-businesses (under ten staff), new businesses and the music sector in general are likely to have approval rates below the average for SMEs as whole.

Banks cite an 80 per cent approval rate for SME loans and overdrafts for Q3 of 2012 [20], yet a Federation of Small Businesses' survey found a 42.8 per cent approval rate for SMEs that applied for bank lending in Q3 2012[21].

The Community Development Finance Association says its members received 3,255 loan applications from 10,475 enquiries, and that 1,540 loans were agreed, of which 60 per cent went to SMEs and 30 per cent to micro-enterprises[22].

4. Investment

Between one and two per cent of applications generally succeed.

Commercial venture capital funds backed by **BIS** have conversion rates of between 0.5 and two per cent of all businesses that approach them actually securing investment[23]. Ingenious Media estimates that fewer than one per cent of businesses that approach them go on to secure funding; most are not suitable for one reason or another[24]. London Business Angels receive "upwards of 800 enquiries per year and funded 17 deals in 2011" (an approximate conversion rate of 2.1 per cent of applications leading to a deal)[25].

TWO

Business Organisation

In the UK, there are a number of ways of choosing to organise a business, the principal ones being sole trader, partnership, private limited company, public limited by company and not-for-profit companies.

There are a number of music activities undertaken, including event production and education that sometimes use a not-for-profit structure. Early consideration of this is advisable because the choice you make about the structure of your business will impact upon what sort of funding you can access.

This chapter will briefly set out the key features of the different forms of business organisation and how these relate to funding. You may want to know what types of funding are open to you as a business, or alternatively whether you should adapt the format structure of your business to fit with the way you plan to fund your business activities.

WAYS OF ORGANISING A BUSINESS

1. Sole Trader

A sole trader is someone who is in business by themselves as a self-employed person. Most musicians or people who are starting out in business operate, initially at least, as sole traders in which capacity you can use a business name, receive money from customers, have employees, set up a business bank account, have business assets and register for VAT.

Imagine that you are Jane Smith, an aspiring music manager. You could offer your management services simply as Jane Smith or you could operate under a trading name such as JS Management. You would have to display who was behind the business, using the styling Jane Smith t/a JS Management on your letterhead and business account – the 't/a' stands for 'Trading As'. As your business grows, you could take on staff. You, Jane Smith, alone, would own the business and consequently have the right to make all the decisions about the business. The administration of the business would be minimal – you could operate as a sole trader using your own bank account, registering as self-employed and simply completing a self-assessment tax return and paying income tax on your business profit. However you would also be responsible for all of the debts and obligations of the business without any limitation on the business liabilities – so if the business went badly and ran into debt or was sued, your own savings, house or property could be taken to pay the business debts. If the business developed and became more complex, at some point you would have to ask the question as to whether you might need to set up a different corporate structure.

2. Partnership

When you find that you want to grow the business and work with some fellow managers, you might choose to go into partnership. You could form a partnership by working together with two other managers and all three of you would become equals in a shared business (rather than employer and employee). You would need to decide with your partners how you will share the ownership, profits, debts and obligations of the business, and how you will take business decisions. You would be taxed in the same ways as a sole trader on your share of the business profits. Bands or music groups often choose a partnership structure for their joint business.

You and your partners might choose to create a written agreement between you, or partnership terms can be agreed verbally. There is no requirement for a written agreement, published accounts or formalised roles, although it might avoid problems later down the line to have details of the partnership recorded in writing for the sake of clarity.

There are some risks here. You, as a partner, will still have personal liability for your joint business; it's just that you share that liability 'jointly and severally' with your fellow partners. If one of them doesn't pay their share of any losses, or makes a bad business decision, you and the remaining partner(s) are personally liable and will have to pay up.

LLP – Another Structure For Partnerships

Fortunately, there is a business structure called the limited liability partnership (LLP), which addresses this issue. An LLP is a hybrid between a partnership and a private limited company allowing members of the partnership to limit their individual liabilities like limited companies can. Members are taxed on their share of the profits, in the same way as a sole trader. This is a relatively new structure, which has been adopted by lots of service firms such as accountancy and legal firms, as well as by bands.

As with a straightforward partnership, you and your partners in the LLP you create will have to decide how you will operate the company. However unlike a general partnership, an LLP has a separate legal identity, distinct from the individual partners who make up its membership. This enables partners to limit their individual liability to the amount, if any, that they agreed with the other partners should the partnership be dissolved.

3. Private Limited Company

So let's assume that JS Management has grown, and you are taking on more liabilities. It's probably then time to set up a limited company, also known as a company limited by shares.

There are two main reasons for setting up a private limited company as opposed to operating as a sole trader or general partnership[1]. As the name suggests, the ability of the directors and shareholders of the company to put a limit on the amount of their own money that can be lost and the degree to which they are legally exposed. Also, incorporation gives the business a separate legal personality set apart from the individual people who are involved in it.

The concept of the 'separate legal personality' of a company is important, and warrants further explanation. Setting up a company is sometimes called 'incorporation', which comes from a Latin word meaning 'to form into a body'. Legally, this means that when you incorporate your business, it becomes an individual body, separated from you, the individual. So while Jane Smith t/a JS Management is an unincorporated business, it has the same legal status as Jane

Smith the person. If you incorporate JS Management Limited, your business becomes, in legal terms, a separate entity, assuming the legal rights, contracts and responsibilities created by the operation of the business. You, Ms Smith, would become a director, shareholder and/or employee of the new company, JS Management Ltd.

What are the benefits of this? If you are taking on a lot of employees, operating activities that carry risk (for example, putting on a tour where there are health and safety issues) or representing artists which may give rise to the potential for legal disputes, you might want to protect yourself by doing this through a limited company structure.

Provided that you act properly within the law as an employee or director, you would not be personally, financially or legally liable for what the company does unless, for example, you chose to give a personal guarantee for the company's debts or bank loans.

The limited company as a business format also allows you to separate the owners (shareholders/ members) from the controllers (the managers) of the business. The ability to do this can build a lot of flexibility into the structure. While the shareholders, directors and managers may be the same individuals at the outset, once you assume this company structure, it permits you to take on additional shareholders who aren't responsible for day-to-day operations, or similarly create directors who do not own shares.

A secondary benefit of establishing a limited company is that the tax arrangements for shareholders can be applied so that you can pay a lower effective rate of tax than if you were, for instance, a sole trader. Shareholders can take a share of the profits of their company via a payment known as a dividend.[2] Dividends are taxed at an effective rate of 10 per cent and are not subject to National

Insurance. Self-employed people, members of partnerships and LLPs pay tax and National Insurance on their profits, so there is a tipping point at which you would keep more of your profits and pay a lower effective tax rate if you were to use the limited company structure and pay yourself a share of the profits through dividends. If they were higher rate taxpayers, shareholders would pay a higher rate of income tax on dividends. However, shareholder directors could also time when they are paid dividends in order to smooth out their income and tax bill.

The benefits of setting up a limited company should be offset against the increased formality and cost of doing so. To create a limited company, you will need a company name and an address at which the company can be contacted (known as a 'registered address'.) You will need to give the name of at least one director and one shareholder (they can be the same individual). Finally you will need to provide details of the company's shares (known as a 'memorandum of association') and rules about how the company is run – known as 'articles of association'. All of this information will need to be sent or uploaded to Companies House, which is the official registry of companies in the UK[3]. It is possible to do this yourself, but most people will ask a company formation agent, accountant or lawyer to do this, as these professionals are very familiar with the procedures involved.

Once the company has been formed there are a number of dates each year when paperwork needs to be filed with Companies House. An important thing to note is that anyone will be able to see a public record of your business at Companies House, find out who the directors of the business are, and obtain a copy of the statutory accounts and records you have filed. Privacy may be a consideration. Small companies can file abbreviated accounts, but larger limited companies and partnerships have to publish detailed accounts.

It will cost a few hundred pounds a year to pay an accountant to prepare your annual accounts, operate your payroll (the procedure for paying yourself and your employees a salary) and file all the paperwork. You will still also have to complete your own self-assessment tax return. However, once you are earning enough for this expense to be less than the additional tax you would pay to operate your business as a sole trader, along with all the benefits of incorporation, it could be worthwhile.

It is best not to overcomplicate things in the beginning. If you are a musician, songwriter or an individual manager, sole trader status is likely to be most appropriate. You can operate under your own name, or a company name if you think that it will help your marketing, branding, professional image or distinctiveness to do so. Unless you are earning reasonable profits or taking on great liabilities, then this is the easiest structure to operate, as it only requires you to declare yourself self- employed to HMRC and complete a self-assessment tax return. It is also easy to combine with other employment you might have, and in the early stages you can offset your business expenses against any tax liability on your self-employed income.

It is more common to set up limited companies for touring, because the short term contracts and extensive public liability can make it worthwhile to do so. There are implications to transferring long-term contracts such as recording and publishing contracts into a limited company, because they have a value as assets that have to be recognised when the transfer is made, and will result in contracts having to be updated. Legal and financial advice should be taken, particularly when dealing with music rights.

4. Public Limited Company

The public limited company (PLC.) structure allows you to sell shares in the company to the public, and for those shares to be traded on the London Stock Exchange[4]. The path to trading shares in a company is a costly one, and would involve a lot of very expensive professional advice. Therefore the PLC. is not going to be used by many, if any, small music companies. It is worth bearing in mind though. If you see your music business as a potentially high-growth company that could attract investment, then the exit strategy of your investors could be that the company will either be sold privately or 'go public' via an 'initial public offering', turning it into a PLC.

5. Not-For-Profit Companies

If your company has socially-minded objectives rather than profit-making ones you might want to set up a different sort of limited company, called a company limited by guarantee. This is sometimes known as a non-profit or not-for-profit limited company. This can be confused with a company that doesn't make any profits or surplus income, which is quite wrong. The company can make a profit, but does not distribute those profits to shareholders because it doesn't have any. The proceeds of the company are normally expected to be used for the benefit of the members or users of the company's services. So most trade associations, for example, are companies limited by guarantee. Directors of non-profit companies are limited in their liability for the company's debts, normally to a fixed value, usually £1. Because the directors do not invest their own money into the company to make a profit, they are not able to take a share of the profits. However if they are working for the company as an employee they may take a salary.

An alternative to a company limited by guarantee would be a charity. A charity might do the same work as a company limited by guarantee, but has certain additional advantages and responsibilities. One of the advantages concerns fundraising: many charities and charitable trusts will only give funding to other charities. Also, many private donors (we aren't going to talk about major donors and philanthropy in this publication) would prefer to give funding when it is clear that it is going to a charity. Charities also benefit from being able to claim Gift Aid[5] on donations and are sometimes exempt from business rates. They have certain responsibilities in return for these benefits. For example, they must set out clear aims and stick to them, and also not do work of a political nature. They are governed by rules set out by the official registrar and regulator of charities in the nation of the UK in which they are based[6].

A community interest company (CIC) is one of a number of other structures that could also be used for 'social enterprises' – it allows the organisation to offer a share of profits to shareholders but keeps the assets in the ownership of the community (hence the name). Its most typical use tends to be for sports clubs or community groups where there are significant assets that they want to protect, but they need private investment to run or to improve them.

FUNDING AND BUSINESS STRUCTURE

When you want to get funding through means other than business trading or committing your own money, the issue of business organisation will be crucial. I will now look at each of the types of funding that will be explored in this book, and what the implications are for business structure.

. . .

1. Grants

Charities are the best-suited structure for grant funding, because many charitable trusts will only award grants to other charities. Very few grants are available to companies limited by shares. For instance, the Arts Council and PRSF grants can be made to profit-making companies provided that they are carrying out a project that is not profit making and which is not the normal business of the company. It is more typical however, that companies limited by guarantee (i.e. not-for-profit) will be among the most likely applicants for arts grants.

There are also some start-up and other business grants from varied sources that might be available to profit-making companies. Grants are often available to individuals, particularly when the money will enable artists to further carry out their work. Arts Council and PRSF again apply here but, in addition, there are also some charitable trusts that specialise in making grants available to individual musicians.

2. Friends and Family

There are no rules here; you can have whatever structure you wish. That said, even with family members, it might be worth establishing the basis for their financial support – are they buying shares? Will they get part of the profits? Are you asking them for a donation or gift? If you were operating as a charity it would be easy to make it clear that it is a donation. If it is a limited company, make it clear whether you are looking for a loan or are offering shares in return for an investment. If you are operating as an individual or sole trader, it's important to define the terms on which they are giving you the money, to avoid potential disputes later on.

· · ·

3. Crowdfunding

Which structure is best for crowdfunding depends on the platform you choose. In order to raise money via Kickstarter[7] for example, you must be a permanent resident of, or a company based in, the UK (or one of the other countries they operate in). Kickstarter's rules specifically forbid charitable campaigns from applying, whereas Indiegogo is open to individuals, businesses and projects as well, and permits a charitable element. It isn't necessary to incorporate in order to use crowdfunding as a mechanism for getting money, but you might feel that the effort that goes into crafting a campaign and the boost you get from having to carefully define your project for your target audience spurs you into wanting to incorporate a company. Furthermore, the boost that a successful campaign can give you can make incorporation worthwhile in terms of quickly growing the project.

4. Sponsorship

Any business form can attract sponsorship, including individuals and sole traders. However, if you are working with a corporate partner who is giving you money, they may prefer you to have a company or charity structure rather than a sole trader structure, confident that an incorporated company is more likely than an individual to reliably fulfil its commitments as part of the sponsorship deal. Sponsors backing an artist may want to work creatively with them, but also have a business representative with whom they can negotiate and hold accountable for the delivery of what they've paid for.

5. Debt Finance

Loans are possible for every business structure, and certainly limited companies and PLCs will make use of overdrafts, mortgages and fixed loans as part of their operations. In practice however, most lenders will require a business loan to be personally guaranteed by the directors or shareholders, particularly if the business does not have an asset (such as property) to secure the loan against.

Banks may insist that a majority shareholder provides a guarantee, even if they are not also a director of the business.

6. Investment

To be able to receive an investment, typically a limited company would be used, normally a profit-making one (although there are some funders willing to invest in social enterprises, LLPs or individuals). An investment made into a company limited by shares means an allocation of shares can be given to the investor. Outside investors can put money into an LLP, and it is possible, although less common, to invest in a sole trader through a specific contract with them.

REGISTERING FOR VAT

Finally, a short note on registering for Value Added Tax (VAT). You must register for VAT when your turnover[8] reaches the threshold of £79,000 (2013/14), whether you are a sole trader, limited company or a non-profit organisation. Don't forget that, as an artist receiving fees and royalties, you may need to charge VAT at the prevailing rate as part of a crowdfunding campaign whereby you are selling items directly to the public, if your overall company turnover reaches the threshold.

It should also be noted that any business structure (including sole trader) might opt to become VAT registered at any level of turnover, not just businesses that reach the mandatory £79,000 threshold. You would have to charge VAT on the goods and services you sell, but would also be able to claim VAT back from goods and services that your company has purchased, such as musical equipment or computers. A detailed explanation is beyond the remit of this guide, and expert financial advice should be sought with respect to the decision on whether or not to register for VAT.

DECIDING HOW TO ORGANISE YOUR BUSINESS

When deciding how best to structure your business, here are some key considerations:

1. Risk

Are you going to be exposed to any risk or assume any liability through providing your services, employing people or agreeing to a contract? If so, how big is the financial risk, what is the chance of the risk occurring and are there any things you can do to mitigate the risk? If something did go wrong, would you be able to meet the liabilities? Do you own any property or assets that could be at risk if a large financial claim were made against you?[9]

If the risk to you is high, and you have a lot to lose, it might be worth incorporating your business as a limited company, either profit making or non-profit, or an LLP.

2. Profit and Ownership

Are you planning to operate as a profit-making business? What is your 'exit strategy' i.e. do you hope to sell the business one day? Do you hope to pay yourself an unlimited amount if the business is very profitable? Would you like to 'own' the business through owning shares? Could the business earn money even if you were not working in it day to day?

If you want to sell the business at some point, would like to seek investment or would like to distribute shares in the company to your employees – basically when things become more involved – a limited company would be worth setting up. If you want to secure investors or tender for public contracts, it will be essential.

Any significant combination of high risks and other factors listed previously should increase your motivation to incorporate your business.

3. Social Aims

Are you carrying out work that you will not be able to make a profit from for ethical reasons or because it will require a subsidy or funding? Do you have social or charitable motivations for carrying out the business? Will you be looking for donations, grants and public sector contracts instead of trading for profit?

If so, then a charity, company limited by guarantee or community interest company could be the right structure. A company limited by guarantee is the simplest to set up, will be familiar to anyone who has been a director of a limited company before, and can be converted later into a CIC or charity. A charity structure is best if you will be generating most of your income through public donations and services to your users, as your charity will not be taxed on this income and can benefit from Gift Aid. A CIC can be limited by shares or by guarantee, so might be a useful structure if you wanted to pay your directors (charity trustees cannot be paid) and have the freedom to trade, but still operate the company for community benefit.

A particular feature of a CIC is the 'asset lock', which means that any assets owned by the company cannot be transferred out for the benefit of directors, but must always be held by a CIC or charity.

FURTHER READING

Running Your Own Business, Kevin Duncan (Hodder Arnold, 2005)

A recommended and no-nonsense guide to running your own business, particularly for service-based businesses. The knowledge and insight shared is also among the most useful and down-to-earth available anywhere, for anyone self-employed.

Entrepreneur: How to Start an Online Business, Lucy Tobin (Capstone, 2012)

Contains great examples of the set-up and growth of many online businesses, and is particularly strong on how business plans change when real- life problems set in.

The Financial Times Guide to Business Start Up 2013 (FT Publishing International, 2012)

An 'old school' guide, if you prefer your guides full of hard factual information.

The Music Management Bible – MMF, Nicola Riches (Editor), (SMT Publishing, 2012)

This includes useful interpretations of joint ventures and other structures concerning artists and managers.

THREE

Grants

It's not commonly known that funding is available for touring, recording, songwriting and marketing, provided you know where to look and even more importantly, how to apply. This chapter begins with two case studies of music industry grant funding – Small Green Shoots, Amplify Dot and Circuit Live (case study A) and Rachel Sermanni, Robert Hicks and Middle Of Nowhere Records (case study B). It then looks at arts councils across the UK (collectively, the single largest source of funding) and the PRS for Music Foundation, and these organisations' music funding policies, with insights from the funders themselves. This chapter also considers the application process with tips from funding insiders, includes pointers for realistic budget preparation and a thorough explanation of the funding relationship. It concludes with a list of key funding organisations.

———

CASE STUDY A: SMALL GREEN SHOOTS, AMPLIFY DOT AND CIRCUIT LIVE

Natalie Wade began her career working as an event organiser for the Urban Music Seminar, a one-time pre-eminent UK conference for urban music. Unaware of arts councils' existence at the time of her own funding search for this event, she was fortunate to receive a direct approach from them, suggesting to her that she could apply to them for conference funding.

From that point on, Wade gained a reputation as the go-to person to help urban musicians and first-time applicants access the grant-funding system.

More recently in 2010, she founded Small Green Shoots (SGS) – a not-for-profit consultancy delivering arts-based projects for 'creatives, corporates and communities'. With clients and partners including corporate brands, local councils, public sector organisations and independent artists, it crafts projects that have a pay-off for artists, brands and grant givers, carefully balancing an artist's ideas and aspirations with the requirements of the funders.

MAKING FUNDING WORK FOR ARTISTS

Wade's skill lies in helping artists who are eligible for grant funding but who are not applying for it due to lack of awareness, knowledge or expertise. This work often begins with facilitating connections, helping develop an artist's work into fundable projects and assisting with funding applications.

"If it fits all the criteria [innovative, exciting, developing music and the people involved in the project] and the priorities of the funder…we'll help the applicant with the language, the system, and the process, to put that bid forward."

This is precisely how SGS helped artist Amplify Dot who impressed the team with her performance skills and focused work ethic. SGS introduced her to management company, Darius Malik Productions. Amplify Dot had ambitions to develop her writing across a range of genres. Combining personal and management company money, a PRS for Music Foundation grant helped provide the balance of the funding required to pay for Amplify Dot's considerable travel expenses incurred in the course of co-writing with a number of prominent writers from British urban genres including Jungle, UK garage and reggae. Wade says:

> "We thought that this project had integrity, it was highly original, and also fitted into what PRSF focus on, which is writing original material."

This funding not only enabled the successful completion of an innovative co-writing project but also lead to other successful outcomes spanning live SGS performances (leading to a subsequent increase in her fanbase), widespread press coverage including featured guest artist in M Magazine [the PRS members' journal] and best of all, becoming the first female UK rapper in a decade to sign an album deal with a major label (Virgin/EMI). Wade told me:

> "That's one we're really proud of, because she really worked for it and she's a great artist."

GETTING OVER THE ASSESSMENT HURDLE

Key to SGS' success is its ability to really understand the funder. Applicants must read the funder's guidelines closely to make sure a project is eligible – ineligibility is one of the most common reasons for failure. Furthermore, the outcome or results of a project will need to be explained in the application, as the funder needs to understand how the project will further its own objectives. The sorts of changes that funders are looking to effect differ, depending on the fund. They can include new songs having being written; the development of artist performance skills (perhaps through mentoring and collaboration); public performances (especially to new audiences which will help build a fanbase for the performer and expose audiences to something they are not necessarily already accessing); and a trial of new ways of working or the creation of work that is progressing the genre or the art form.

Wade stresses that the project-based nature of most funding means that funders want to see how an applicant will deliver a specific project and typically don't allow funding to be used to prop up the regular overhead costs of running a company (general telephone, insurance, equipment etc.). So while rent and wages can't usually be claimed for, paying for a project administrator would be allowable as it's a short-term, project-specific cost. The same would be true for studio hire costs for the duration of the project, for example.

Ultimately, both funding outcomes and funding criteria can vary from funder to funder.

The relationship with the funder is also significant. Wade talks about the importance of writing for the 'assessor', the person or people who will be reading your application and the others competing for it. They might have a heavy workload of applications to consider. Here's her advice:

> "Think like you're writing to the assessor personally… about what she needs to see and how quickly she needs to see it, so be succinct. Create an image in her head of what this might look like. Give a story, show a legacy 'with this money, this event/project/ creation will happen' and convey what lasting effect might it have."

The concept, and then the details requested – budget, marketing plan, project plan – need to be presented clearly and concisely so that there is no impediment to the assessor approving the application.

ONE FUNDER LEADS TO ANOTHER

Working with multiple funders and using match funding[1] is also part of the method that most organisations working with public funding deploy. It means that individual funders are exposed to less risk because there are several organisations each committing a proportion of the money. Also, support from one funder can make other funders more willing to come on board.

An example of this was an SGS music event that took place as a 'pop-up' street festival. Some funding was awarded from the local council, with other funding made by PRSF, because it met their funding criteria for festivals (they are eligible from the second time a festival is staged).

> "Whenever we're working with organisations, or events, or
> companies, we always go to the local council and say: 'Look,
> would you invest in this? Would you put some money behind it –
> even if it's just £200–300?'"

A council's backing shows that an event is really wanted in the local
area; it demonstrates a need or public benefit. It's not just about the
artist or a project.

Small Green Shoots' Circuit Live project is a complex example of
this, involving five spoken word artists (including Ty and Rodney P)
delivering a literature workshop for young people based on Olympic
and Paralympic values. The workshops took place across five
London boroughs, inside local libraries. It involved various youth
organisations and drew young music fans who might not ordinarily
be interested in literature, into those libraries, concluding with a
performance at the British Library that was reported on by the
Evening Standard.

The project was a funding success story because it was match
funded and involved so many partners, which meant that for a
modest budget it was able to deliver multiple benefits: artists were
paid to do their work; young people were encouraged into libraries;
50 young people earned bronze Arts Awards; and the boroughs,
libraries and youth projects had a well-developed, high-quality event
that tied in with the Olympics and achieved positive press coverage
for the artists, funders and partners involved.

Going forward, it is part of the SGS mission to continue to find
creative ways of funding work with artists in what is a challenging
and competitive environment.

NATALIE WADE'S TIPS ON APPLYING FOR FUNDING

1. Think about the assessor

The person reading your application. They will probably have to score you against their criteria, so make sure you have given them the information as clearly and succinctly as possible so they can give you a clear 'tick' against those boxes.

2. Consider match funding

This is a way to strengthen the application and reduce your reliance on one pot of money.

3. Spend some time on writing

Take time writing the application, including drafting and redrafting what you have written. If possible, get the funder to look at a draft... or a friend... or someone who has successfully applied before. Make sure it is easy to read and understand, and is well formatted. Consider the use of bullet points, tables or lists where this could make the application easier to scan.

4. Carefully consider the timeline

If there is a six- week turn around for your application and your funded activity is supposed to occur eight weeks after you apply, your ability to deliver the project in time might be in doubt.

5. Demonstrate your credibility and track record

This can be with letters of support; by detailing the credentials of the partners in your project; press coverage; or evidence of past successes. This can be useful if the funder is not so familiar with your work.

. . .

6. Public Benefit

Think about the public benefit and the benefit to the wider art form – in the case of public money, this is important.

7. Quality

Demonstrate the quality of your work artistically, if the funders prioritise this. This may mean sending good quality recordings and copies of reviews.

8. Keep your integrity

If your project really doesn't fit with a funder's criteria, don't fundamentally change it in order to fit.

————

CASE STUDY B: RACHEL SERMANNI AND ROBERT HICKS, MIDDLE OF NOWHERE RECORDS

Robert Hicks has a background in music promotion with his Highlands-based company, Beyond. He is something of a serial entrepreneur, having an interest in festivals, a pub and other related businesses. Speaking to him, he is emphatic that his entry into managing artists and a record label was not part of his plans. His company was booking Scottish singer-songwriter Rachel Sermanni for shows, and, feeling that she was an exceptional talent, he began introducing her to experienced managers. However in the meantime, Hicks became increasingly convinced that he could take on the job of managing Sermanni:

> "A friend, Ben, from Mumford and Sons who is a massive fan and supporter of Rachel said 'you should do it' and I suppose that gave

us the confidence, but we were still very nervous. Rachel wanted to find her own path and I always felt that I was there to support what she wanted to do, rather than pushing her in a certain direction."

THE BOTHY SESSIONS

As part of her development, Sermanni and Hicks made an application to Creative Scotland for a grant of around £2,000 to make their first live recording, which resulted in *The Bothy Sessions* EP. Hicks recalls how the project was implemented:

"Rachel sent a text message out to about twenty musician friends, and said, 'I'm going to do a recording, is anyone up for taking part? We're going to make an EP, you've got to be at Aviemore station in two days time, if you're interested.' About a dozen turned up in the end, they walked two miles into the hills, to a bothy[2]. They hadn't heard the songs, so they spent a day rehearsing and then recorded into the mic and we ended up with our first EP. That's what Creative Scotland supported... for the creative process it was very enriching for everyone."

The grant meant that they were able to pay for an engineer, mastering and pressing costs, therefore creating a better quality end product than would have otherwise been possible.

The EP campaign was highly targeted, given the small budget, involving select servicing to national and local radio, and regional press. As a result, it soon sold out of its limited run. At this point, the project, as funded by Creative Scotland, came to an end.

However the benefits to the artist have continued, and after several re-pressings, The Bothy Sessions EP had sold 3,500 copies, providing valuable cash flow for the young artist's business.

BUILDING THE LABEL

Sermanni followed this up by recording and self-releasing the *Black Currents* EP as a studio recording, achieving a number one in the UK independent chart, which in turn helped to build her profile. She then formed Middle of Nowhere Records and in September 2012 put out the *Under Mountains* LP, which sold over 7,000 copies, according to Hicks.

When the team had made and released Under Mountains, and were planning a European tour, they were able to apply to Creative Scotland for tour support. Hicks says:

> "Again we went to Creative Scotland to support the release with a contribution to her European touring and when we released the record in Europe we were able to recruit a press person in every country to which she was touring. The whole tour was a considerable financial undertaking ... the grant was instrumental in making it happen, engaging press companies allowed us to maximise the results."

SIGNIFICANT IMPACT

Hicks states that the overall impact of the grants received has been vital to the development of Sermanni's career:

> "The grants have come along at very fortunate and opportune times. When we [recorded] The Bothy Sessions the timing was

right for her to do something, but it would have put a strain on us financially. After the album campaign, when we decided to go ahead and do it ourselves, it made a massive difference to Rachel's visibility in other European countries. We are a little bedroom indie label, but we always wanted to do it properly and employ radio, press and online teams and fully service it. We can only cash flow that in the UK ourselves."

So the grants have clearly had a significant impact on the ability of the small label to present a professional image. Of course the application process can be challenging, especially if you are new to it. Hicks says:

"I find the application process the hardest thing in the world. We are a very small team – it takes so much time and I'm not very good at writing them. For a small cottage industry, to spend days trying to write an application if you are only going for a tiny amount of support [can be frustrating]. If you [learn to speak the right language] it is all straightforward, it's just getting your head realigned."

It is clear that the support of Creative Scotland has been invaluable, and it's something that the artist and her manager would do again in the future, if the business required it.

———

WHAT IS A GRANT?

A grant is an amount of money that does not have to be repaid, but the grant giving organisations will expect something in return. A few examples of specific requirements that funders require of recipients are that they meet their aims, acknowledge the funding, report on progress, to work on a project basis and demonstrate 'additionality'.

1. Meeting Their Aims

Each grant giver has aims or principles that determine what they fund and they also have conditions that determine how their money is distributed. The RVW Trust was established by composer Ralph Vaughan Williams in 1956, and provides an example of this. The Trust says:

> "He had always been a generous personal supporter of many musical and charitable purposes and he wanted to ensure that this support could continue after his death... the income from the performing rights in his music could be directed towards the purposes which he held dear."

In this case, the charity is likely to be receptive towards grant applications seeking to stage performances of little performed 19th and 20th century composers. We'll look at the aims of other funders later in this chapter.

2. Acknowledgement

The grant giver will want their funding to be explicitly acknowledged by you, and perhaps to be able to use the results of your funded project in their own publicity.

3. Reporting

As with all other types of funder, grant givers will require accountability and feedback, in the form of reporting or evaluation of the work. The governing boards of trustees within charities typically require a written report showing that the grants they've

awarded have been appropriately spent, in line with the application
that was approved.

4. Working on a project basis

Grants tend to be offered based on a pitch for a particular project
and most charities are reluctant to fund general overheads (e.g. rent,
rates and power) or administration costs, although these can
sometimes be included where they are specific to the project.
Therefore, grant givers typically expect to see a beginning and end
date to the work, so that they know that recipients are not going to
be dependent on their funding on an on-going basis.

5. Additionality

This curious term means that grant givers expect you to show that
your project wouldn't ordinarily have been carried out, or
implemented to the same standard, without the benefit of grant
funding. The use of their grant must be seen to be making a
difference and be in addition to what you might already be able to
achieve with your own resources.

Although grant givers do want something in return for their
funding, there are distinct advantages to grants. They are a type of
funding based on motivations other than profit. This means they
can be a better fit than investment or loans for some of the cultural
work that music companies or musicians might want to do.

Another advantage is that grant givers generally publish transparent
information about who and what they will fund, and offer written
guidance that makes it easier to tailor your application to their aims,
increasing the likelihood of eligibility and success.

It is worth noting that, as with all funding, relationships, lobbying
and personal preferences do play some part in the allocation of

grant funding. It could be argued that these biases are unfair, but it is natural that grant givers will develop on-going relationships with certain recipients. Michael Phillips' book The Seven Laws of Money[3] describes this as an 'alliance' between the trust or grant giving body and the recipient, whereby the grant giving organisation derives a number of additional benefits from supporting certain recipients, over and above that recipient simply delivering their project. Phillips says that with these recipients the grant giver can get ideas for future projects, develop their fund in new areas, inform their strategy, gain kudos, enjoy a good working relationship and so on. These alliances result in some grant givers working with certain recipients repeatedly, and even designating funds with specific recipients in mind. If the grant- giver wants to fund a new area of work, they occasionally allocate funds directly without the preferred recipient needing to apply for general funds, or set the criteria in such a way that the preferred applicants can easily tailor their bid to suit.

WHERE CAN YOU GET GRANTS?

The bodies that give the most substantial grants to music in the United Kingdom are Arts Council England, Arts Council Wales, Arts Council Northern Ireland, Creative Scotland and PRS for Music Foundation.

I will focus in detail on the music grants offered by these organisations because, due to their size, scope and relevance to the majority of musicians and music companies, they constitute the best starting point for most first-time applicants. Finally, this chapter provides a list of a wide range of charitable trusts and grant giving organisations that specialise in music.

With regards to the four arts councils: each one has the status of a non-departmental public body that is allocated money from its respective government. There is therefore a requirement on them to fund key institutions and broadly reflect government policy on the arts, as well as developing the arts on behalf of the country. All of the UK's arts councils offer funding for individual artists and organisations to carry out artistic projects. They all offer at least three modes of funding – open-access funds (like England's Grants for the Arts funding)[4], regular funding for organisations that are important to the nation's arts 'ecosystem', and strategic or managed funds which are set aside for specific strategic purposes.

Because all the arts councils operate similar modes of funding, to avoid repetition, I have given more detail about the way funding works in the section on Arts Council England, before describing more briefly the national variations in Wales, Northern Ireland and Scotland under their own separate headings. The application techniques described apply to all four nations, however.

1. Arts Council England (ACE)

There are a number of pots of money administrated by ACE that relate to music. I will outline the following schemes that I consider to be key for music: Grants for the Arts (GftA), The National Music Portfolio, Momentum Music (The Artist Development Fund) and Creative Industry Finance.

I will not cover the funding for Music Education Hubs[5] in England, which is distributed by ACE (although many musicians may ultimately be paid for their teaching work through music education hubs) because these are administrated in a variety of ways depending on their geographical location, and discussion of them is beyond the scope of this book.

a. Grants for the Arts

Most musicians and music organisations can apply directly to a scheme called Grants for the Arts (GftA). This is a fund of money from the UK National Lottery of which £6.6 million in 2011/12 went to music. The awards were between £1,000 and £250,000 each. Over half of the actual grants awarded were under £10,000.

There is a common misunderstanding about who can receive grants, which needs to be addressed. Many of the people I spoke to in the course of my research for this book said something like: "I can't apply for funding because I am not a charity, and I am not doing something worthy". Grants can actually be used by individual artists and also by limited companies: applicants do not have to be charities. While the projects themselves cannot be profit-making, the companies that are applying for the funding can be, and the artists who receive funding are, in fact, supposed to pay themselves out of their funding.

I interviewed Arts Council England's Music Director Penny King, who says that because GftA is Lottery money, it does need to be clear how the project will reach an audience. King says:

> "It's really about [the artist] making a case for what they want to do… artistically and how that benefits the public, including the benefit to them [the artist] and their development."

It is also important, according to King, that applicants think about the reason for applying for funding in the first place:

> "Framing it in the context of a project… just about any company model can apply [to ACE]… but what they really need to show is that the project that they're applying for is something that couldn't

happen without public funding, and that, in itself, needs the funding."

So if a project were within the capacity of the applicant to fund themselves, or to deliver on a profit-making basis, it wouldn't be suitable for funding. On the other hand, a profit-making company that applies for funding to undertake a specific project that it wouldn't be able to produce profitably, but which will be artistically excellent and something that audiences wouldn't have otherwise been able to see, will be considered. Penny King added:

> "There aren't enough actual artists applying... they're not necessarily looking towards the opportunities that the Arts Council might offer to help them develop what they do."

In my experience, the idea of filling in these grant application forms is something that many artists find off-putting or intimidating. However, applying for a grant is actually relatively straightforward compared to many of the funding opportunities covered in this guide, and artists certainly should apply if they feel they have a project that could and should be funded.

Later in this chapter, you will find examples of typical Grants for the Arts projects that illustrate the types of projects that all arts councils tend to fund, and a sample budget.

Applicants in England should download the detailed list of what was funded in the previous year, for reference, in addition to reading the guidelines for recordings, if recording will be a part of a project.

Be sure to check the guidelines for preparing a Grants for the Arts application, which are available from the ACE website.

. . .

b. The National Music Portfolio

National portfolio organisations (NPOs) are so called because together they form part of what ACE intends to be a balanced portfolio of arts organisations, across different art forms, regions and sizes. An NPO is allocated funding from ACE over a two or three-year period against a planned programme of work, and the money normally pays for some of what are called 'core costs' or overheads, such as staff salaries, office rent and administration costs. This is intended to give the NPOs stability to develop artistic work and find further funding for their activities. There are occasionally new NPOs, which are likely to be organisations that have already successfully applied for GtfA and are well-established companies. There are NPOs in all areas of the arts.

In music, ACE will award £213 million over the three years 2012–15, to 84 music organisations. To further illustrate the balance of the portfolio, 85–90 per cent of the funding goes to symphony orchestras, opera and other classical music organisations involved with festivals and recording. The remaining 10–15 per cent is shared between organisations in a variety of musical styles such as jazz, African, Asian and popular music. In terms of size, the NPOs range from organisations of national and international importance such as the English National Opera (£54 million, the largest amount given to an NPO), Sage Gateshead (10.8 million) and Bournemouth Symphony Orchestra (£7.8 million). Smaller NPOs include Serious Events Ltd (promoters of the London Jazz Festival, £1.38m), British Underground (a partner in the British Music Abroad Scheme that helps subsidise musicians to attend showcases like South By South West (SXSW), £458,000) and NMC Recordings (a charity that records and promotes work by British composers with £120,000 – the smallest amount that can be given to an NPO).

Many music companies and musicians might enjoy secondary benefits from funding through the arts councils, by way of free or subsidised training, advice, rehearsal and recording space, performance opportunities and commissions.

For applicants in England, a full list of music NPOs and how much funding they receive is available from the ACE website, and is worth reading in order to get a sense of the ways in which ACE funding has been applied to music.

c. Momentum Music (Artist Development Fund)

ACE has recognised that its funds and application process may be perceived by artists as inaccessible. It may be that artists feel that funding is for larger organisations, and indeed that is where the majority of the funding goes; or maybe they think of themselves as part of the commercial music business and therefore not fitting the profile of 'the arts' that ACE literature refers to.

In particular, many voices from the music industry have recommended that it would be useful to have a scheme that specifically addresses the need for the development of 'contemporary popular music'.

Alan Davey, the CEO of ACE recognised this in an attention-grabbing blog-post on the Huffington Post in early 2012 in which he wrote:

> "Perhaps it's time to look at new ways of micro-financing recording and promoting emerging musicians – whether by loans or grants – and making sure that talent has time to mature and develop. Any plan to do this would need to offer support in nimble and flexible ways, and would need to involve and be backed by the

music industry… so while many reports on the fate of the music industry focus on the bottom line, we need to start a debate about how together we can support the development of artists in the longer term. Invention, innovation and a long-term view will be essential if we're to keep the music industry interesting as well as profitable, and for talent to emerge and be sustained."

In response to this thinking, ACE has developed an artist development fund called Momentum Music, worth £500,000 over two years, and administrated by PRS for Music Foundation. This fund is a pilot for ACE specially devised as a new way of funding music. It has several merits. While the GftA fund has a relatively lengthy application process and a six-week turnaround time, with this fund, PRSF will use an application process that is less daunting for exactly the sort of artists that ACE wants its money to reach. For example, in 2012 PRSF started to use a two-stage application process whereby artists submitted some music and brief information at the first stage. If the music and concept were strong enough (in the opinion of a panel of assessors) they would progress to the second stage, knowing that it would be worthwhile writing and developing a full application. More detail about this novel application process is provided later in this chapter.

By working through an organisation that is seen as more connected to the artist and the commercial music industry, ACE's money will more easily reach, as Penny King calls it:

"the creative economy beyond the traditional arts – beyond the sort of traditional boundaries that people have seen with the Arts Council."

Whilst recognising that popular music needs this kind of support, ACE's own funding (i.e. administration and grant-in-aid budgets) has been reduced by government, and the organisation has to work creatively to maximise the impact of its money. This fund is an opportunity to co-fund (with PRSF and the music industry or private individuals) artist development at this level. This scheme is also, in an indirect way, supporting the small companies that are such a strength of the British music industry. King says:

> "It's testing a mechanism for encouraging artists to seek support at a fairly low level. We're talking about £5,000 to £15,000 so it's not absolute entry level; it's for people who've got a bit of a track record and who already have a foot on the ladder in terms of a career. A relatively small sum of money that can significantly help them develop their music."

Ultimately, obtaining the funding is dependent on the artist producing a business plan showing how funding will significantly impact their career progression. It is also necessary to provide evidence of what has already been achieved in terms of building a fanbase and securing representation or partnerships within the music industry. At least 10 per cent of the money for the planned activity, be it recording, touring or marketing, will have to be provided by the artist. There are four deadlines per year for the fund, and responses will be given within six weeks of each deadline.

d. Creative Industry Finance

Another ACE initiative focused on support for the 'Creative Industries' as opposed to 'The Arts' is the Creative Industry Finance programme.

The pilot programme was devised and delivered by ArtCo Trading Ltd (a subsidiary company of Arts Council England) in partnership with the East London Small Business Centre and The Key Fund in Yorkshire. Creative Industry Finance (CIF) gives free business support to small-scale creative businesses, not just in music, although the idea began with thinking about how to support music companies. Launched in May 2012, CIF runs until at least the end of March 2014. In May 2013, responsibility for the delivery and development of this programme was transferred from ArtCo Trading Ltd (along with the staff and assets) to Creative Sector Services CIC, a new independent community interest company that is funded by Arts Council England.

This fund is designed to offer targeted support for both early stage and more established businesses that need to access finance in order to grow. Successful applicants are offered up to 12 hours of business support leading to an application for funding which is presented to a loan panel. Applicants must have been trading for at least six months and have been turned down for a loan from their own bank before they are eligible to apply for a Creative Industry Finance loan. Penny King says:

> "This is about trying to support people who are finding it difficult to get investment through the normal mechanisms but who have real potential. The process can lead to an application for finance through the scheme that is interest bearing – currently 10 per cent APR – and payable back over a certain period. So a certain number of people will get investment but a lot more will get the business support and advice leading up to it."

Bryony Beynon, who works on the Creative Industry Finance programme, says that so far the scheme has funded 32 businesses, with seven recipients from the music sector. The loans they were given were mainly for expansion of existing businesses, and included a music studio, a songwriting training company, music software firms and a live music promoter. At the time of writing, plans were being developed to rollout the initiative nationally.

2. Arts Council of Wales (ACW)

As with all Arts Councils, ACW has a portfolio of strategically important national music organisations, to which it provides 'revenue funding'. Revenue funded organisations (RFOs) receive their money on an annual basis, and can use it to pay for core running costs and salaries as well as project costs. The 12 music organisations in the RFO portfolio share £6.8 million of revenue funding between them. By far the largest of the organisations in the portfolio is the Welsh National Opera, with an annual grant of £4.75 million.

Arts Council of Wales is also a distributor of Lottery funds. Arts grants for individuals and organisations based in Wales are also available for research and development, creating new work for production or touring, training, mentoring and continuing professional development, and business and market development. Individuals can apply for small grants of £5,000, or less at any time, with larger grants awarded four times per year. Typically, Arts Council of Wales funding will pay a maximum of 90 per cent of costs (depending on the fund), so at least 10 per cent of the money will need to be found from another source to match this.

The total amount that went to music organisations and individuals working in music through these schemes in the financial year 2012/13 was just over £2.6 million, with individual grants ranging from £600 up to £100,000. The typical amount was £5,000, probably because this is the upper limit for ACW's small grants that can be applied for at any time.

One of the most notable things about Arts Council of Wales' strategy is that it currently has music industry development as one of its main funding priorities. It wants to support new models and help create a sustainable music sector, echoing the Welsh Government's support for music and creative industries, which includes its core funding of the Welsh Music Foundation as a support agency for music industry in the nation.

As Arts Council of Wales' strategy document states:

> "Music industry development grants are uniquely available to organisations working in the music industry in Wales. And they're designed to meet some specific needs."

The funding is meant to be targeted at artists at a:

> "Tipping point in their career or development path asking for investment for a fundamental change to what they do in order to take them up to the next level".

Therefore Arts Council of Wales requires a business plan that shows how the funding will be used to really impact the applicant's business. It needs to go beyond simply making a recording. ACW's wider strategy is to enable music companies and musicians to retain their intellectual property and actively exploit their creative work. Projects that are likely to be funded are those that provide a product or performance for which there is audience demand, performing at industry showcases internationally, developing new business models and increasing partner investment.

Lisa Matthews, Portfolio Manager at Arts Council of Wales says that its commitment to music industry development is intended to ensure that it does a better job of reaching the non-classical and opera music genres. This strategy, she says, has proved successful:

"It's been a really useful way to get new people to come forward. That's where it all came from, an understanding that we wanted to support the music sector beyond opera and orchestral music, realising that the 'contemporary' sector was facing its own challenges. It worked as we get people in bands and music enterprises phoning us up having heard of the music industry development funding. The conversation can often lead to a different fund, such as training or the artist loans scheme."

Arts Council of Wales' strategy also includes a 'designated priority' for festivals. It has been instrumental in bringing the WOMEX 2013 world music convention to Cardiff, and is closely involved as a partner in that project. It also works with colleagues in the Welsh Government's Major Events Unit to support a number of music festivals. The Government is responsible for supporting creative business, with Arts Council of Wales responsible for the artistic element, but they work together to do this in a 'holistic' way, says Matthews. Examples of this include their joint support for the Huw Stephens' curated SWN festival, Green Man and Focus Wales. She says:

"Our support looks at the arts offer, [specifically] how a festival might raise the profile of Welsh talent and give [that talent] access to the audience that the festival might have been developing for years. Also [consideration is given to] the public benefit of such festivals – from getting to experience new music to outreach work and skills development. The Major Event Unit's focus is on the economic impact of an event and the opportunity to see Wales in a positive way. In times of austerity, the emerging or riskier bookings can be the first thing to get cut, so we're keen to see that the talent doesn't get cut back."

ACW's interest-free loans for artists support 20 to 30 artists each year with their professional costs including workspace, materials and marketing expenses. Finally, alongside the support for training included in the arts grants scheme, ACW provides a fund for advanced (postgraduate) music study for musicians from Wales.

3. Arts Council Of Northern Ireland (ACNI)

ACNI distributes funding for arts in Northern Ireland and also has a fund for creative industries development. In 2013/14 it will award over £13 million to arts projects in Northern Ireland. As with other national arts councils it funds key institutions with its largest music client Ulster Orchestra (awarded £2.19 million in 2012/13), and it also supports arts centres such as The MAC in Belfast, which provides a music programme.

ACNI recently launched its five-year music strategy for the period 2013–17, including some important changes as to how the organisation approaches music. As part of this strategy, it acknowledges that while the organisation is "firmly committed to enabling people in Northern Ireland to experience the best music in any form", its research indicates "the need for a far more inclusive approach to the diversity of genres and different musics". In response, by way of example, ACNI will develop a touring scheme that will give priority to jazz, chamber, world and contemporary music. Also, following on from Derry/Londonderry being the UK City of Culture 2013, it will develop a multi-agency strategy for supporting festivals.

ACNI already operates a number of schemes for helping talented young musicians from school-aged to early professional level access to musical instruments and training (Musical Instrument Scheme; NIOpera; Milton Violin Award; ACNI Young Artists Programme and Support for the Individual Artists Programme). However, the new strategy will open these up to a wider range of genres. The ACNI Young Artists Programme, which allows applicants to spend time learning from a master teacher, will now be widened to include traditional music and jazz as well as classical. There will also be 'greater support for travel awards in the cause of professional development', meaning that it should be possible to access funding for performances outside of Northern Ireland and for training.

Most exciting, perhaps, is the strategic priority to:

> "Commit, along with Invest NI and other stakeholders, to a long-term joint strategic programme for the music industry, and ensure our contribution is consistent with our core purpose of supporting the creation and performance of music and the promotion of that music to audiences."

This strategy should help leverage more financial and in-kind support for diverse genres of music.

Clearly the ACNI is in the middle of making some carefully planned changes to its music portfolio, which will reshape the availability of its funding to contemporary music companies and musicians.

There are two specific funds worth highlighting to music companies. The first is the Creative Industries Innovation fund, which funded 133 creative businesses in Northern Ireland between 2008–11, and will reopen for a second round of applications in January 2014. The second is the Small Grants scheme, which is open to not-for- profit organisations, and operates similarly to Arts Council England's Grants for the Arts programme. This distributes many small grants of between £500 and £10,000 for delivering creative projects, including performances.

4. Creative Scotland

In Scotland, the situation is slightly different. The national opera, ballet, orchestra and theatre companies are funded directly from government and not via an arms-length organisation. Creative Scotland is the national organisation that supports the arts, screen and creative industries.

Creative Scotland distributes National Lottery and Scottish Government funding in a number of different ways. While there isn't a music sector specific scheme in Scotland as there is in Wales and England, most of the funding schemes it operates are open to music projects. Funding programmes include long-term funded foundation organisations such as Fèisean nan Gaidheal and Fèis Rois, the umbrella association of the Fèis movement, which provide music activities, performances and music tuition that reach thousands of young people and audience members each year.

Programme Funded Organisations are another group of beneficiaries of Creative Scotland's funding, that focus on the production, presentation and distribution of work and which are supported with funding for up to two years. Music organisations supported in this way include the Scottish National Jazz Orchestra and Hands up for Trad; the latter being dedicated to increasing the profile and visibility of Scottish traditional music. There are 16 Foundation and Programme organisations that work primarily in music. In 2012–13 Creative Scotland's budget for these organisations was £2.4 million. A further seven venues or organisations whose work is cross- art form, but include significant music activity, had a total budget of £1.3 million from Creative Scotland. There are also annual clients that are funded on a year-to-year basis to provide services and support networks for the arts and broader creativity in Scotland. The National Youth Orchestras of Scotland, Enterprise Music Scotland, Scottish Music Industry Association, Scottish Music Centre and Scottish Jazz Federation are all annual clients.

For readers of this guide, funding is also available through a series of open funding programmes for individuals and organisations to develop and deliver projects. There is support to create new music, to record, to tour, for research and training and other professional development; to explore overseas opportunities; to tour and showcase overseas; for music residencies and for talent development; for companies who work in the digital music sector and for music companies who wish to grow their businesses.

Support is also given for a series of major events in Scotland which feature music and for showcases of Scottish musical talent at the Edinburgh Festivals. However, this support is spread over a number of funding schemes.

Music and music-based projects make up a large portion of a number of the awards, particularly in schemes like Quality Production, which enables artists to create new work, and in the International Fund, which supports artists to develop new markets overseas. Creative Scotland supports musicians to professionally record and release their music, through the Quality Production Fund, and this remains one of the most successful investments in the music sector. Increasingly Scottish artists are retaining their own intellectual property (IP) as a result of such investments and are licensing their recordings or self-releasing and therefore retaining a larger share of the income. The Innovation Fund has supported a significant number of music companies who are creating innovative digital content, inventive ways for people to engage with this as well as new business-models to support their development.

International showcasing is also a significant area of activity with showcases at South by South West (SXSW), Australasian World Music Expo, Celtic Colours in Cape Breton, and Folk Quebec in Montreal, Canada. Showcase Scotland at Celtic Connections, (Glasgow's annual winter music festival) is the largest gathering of the international music community in Scotland and showcases a selection of the country's talent to promoters, record labels and agents. Music festivals are a major part of the Scottish festivals calendar and Creative Scotland supports many including Celtic Connections, St Magnus Festival, the Hebridean Celtic Festival and SOUND.

Creative Scotland also plays a key role in supporting music education via the Youth Music Initiative and also in the skills and training arena via the provision of paid graduate internships in music companies. The Youth Music Initiative (YMI) is currently funded £10 million per annum, with £8 million being routed from Scottish Government through Creative Scotland to local authorities into schools to ensure that all children receive the opportunity of one year's music tuition by the end of their primary school education.

5. PRS for Music Foundation (PRSF)

PRSF was established in 2000. Its inauguration formalised and made transparent a history of the Performing Right Society (now PRS for Music) funding the creation of new music, a policy it had been operating on a discretionary basis since 1953.

The formation of PRSF followed plans by PRS for Music to abolish its classical music subsidy in 1998. At the time, classical music compositions earned a higher rate for public performances than compositions and songs in other genres. Publishers and writers from non-classical genres argued that their income was being used to subsidise the classical sector, and that the costs of classical publishers investing in new music was no greater than those of popular music publishers. Those supporting the subsidy countered that a lot of the income going to the estates of major writers such as Britten, Holst and Vaughn Williams was actually given away in grants, but again this argument did not meet the criticism that only the classical music sector was being supported. Eventually, it was agreed to simultaneously abolish the classical subsidy and establish the PRS for Music Foundation to give grant funding to all music genres, with an initial grant of £1 million per year.

PRSF is now supported by a grant of £1.5 million per year from PRS for Music, on a rolling three-year basis, which it augments with funding from the arts councils, trusts, foundations and individuals. Vanessa Reed, Executive Director of the PRSF says:

> "Any other funder who sees [there is] support from PRS for Music Foundation knows that [the project has] been approved by music experts and that would seem to have real value in addition to the money itself. So I think our brand is… almost as important as our money, enabling lots of the people we fund to lever additional resources from other funders."

As previously stated, part of the reason for creating a foundation was to make PRS for Music's grant giving more efficient and more transparent. The PRSF funds individuals, groups and organisations. Broadly, what it funds is the creation of new music to be performed live. It also has specific funds for international showcasing, artist development and female composers, and 21 funds for commissions and music creation that operate in partnership with other organisations. The organisation has made great efforts to make the application process as simple as possible; this is outlined in detail later in the chapter. Reed says:

> "Our on-going strategy is always to support the very best of those making, creating and promoting new music in the UK, and we support the breadth of the music industry in the UK. This led us to actually changing our assessment processes and selection criteria… our focus is listening to the music through clips that are submitted as part of the application forms and we think that's now more important than reading the words [on an application] form because we know that the best artists aren't always the best at filling in forms."

The Foundation has also increasingly tried to develop a balanced portfolio of projects. Reed further explains:

> "In terms of the diversity and breadth of what we fund, we've always been careful to look at how much of our grant goes to Scotland, Northern Ireland, Wales and England, and how much is going to different music genres, whether that be urban, folk, classical, jazz etc."

Two specific examples of PRSF funding are the British Music Abroad scheme and funding for individuals, organisations and groups.

a. British Music Abroad Scheme

This scheme has been specifically targeted at popular music for a number of years. Run by the partner organisations PRSF, British Underground, UK Trade & Investment and Arts Council England, the British Music Abroad scheme offers support for artists to reach a worldwide audience. It is open to any artists based in the UK who have been invited (i.e. have applied and been accepted) to perform at an industry-facing showcase or festival such as Eurosonic, SXSW, WOMEX and so on. 10 per cent of all applications to the scheme are successful. Examples of artists recently funded under this scheme are Luke Sital-Singh, SOHN and Mary Epworth.

b. Funding For Individuals, Organisations And Groups

These are the 'core' funding schemes for PRS for Music Foundation, which are funded from its annual grant from PRS for Music. The individuals, organisations and groups it funds must apply for a specific project (a one-off activity) or programme (series of activities) that meets the aims of the organisation: to support the creation and performance of outstanding new music in any genre, to develop artists to their full potential and to inspire audiences. Typical applicants are songwriters, festival promoters or organisations that commission new music to be written and performed. The scheme can't support profit-making companies, such as record companies, but it can support an individual artist. The cost of making demos and recordings are not supported through the core fund, although in the context of a wider project the costs of working with a producer could be covered. You must have been operating as an individual or organisation for at least 18 months.

These are open schemes, meaning anyone eligible may apply. There are deadlines four times each year when applications can be submitted. The turnaround time following stage one in terms of feedback is around four weeks following the deadline, and a further eight if an applicant reaches stage two; there is therefore a 12 week wait from deadline to outcome for a successful application.

Typical examples of the kinds of projects funded are:

• a commission for a composer or songwriter to write a new piece of music for performance

• a tour

• a festival programme

• a composer residency

• a series of live events

• an education project

• artist development

Here are three specific examples of PRSF supported projects:

Writer Commissioned To Make A New Piece Of Music

PRSF funded the Youth Music Theatre to commission a new musical, Loserville, from Elliot Davis and James Bourne. This meant that the organisation had funds to pay the writers and were able to develop the work for performance at the West Yorkshire Playhouse. The musical has since gone on to open in London's West End.

Artist Developing Their Music For A Live Performance

PRSF funded electronic music artist James Birchall (aka Rough Fields) to arrange and rehearse his music with a band, in order to be able to perform it live on tour.

.　.　.

A Festival Programme

PRSF funded East London promoters Sexbeat to stage their one-day festival Radfest so that new music from UK artists could be performed live. Around 80 per cent of the PRSF grant money goes to organisations and groups (including bands) and 20 per cent to individual applicants. This also reflects the percentage of applicants to each scheme, which is around 80/20 at each deadline. First-time applicants may apply for up to £5,000. Those who have been funded in previous years may apply for up to £25,000.

The average proportion of applications that receive some sort of funding is 15 per cent, and in 2012 52 per cent of successful applicants received the full amount they applied for. In order to maximise the number of good projects that it can fund, PRSF encourages people to apply only for the amount they need, and to disclose any other income related to their project.

The PRSF additionally offers limited partnership funds from time to time such as the New Music 20x12 programme, Composer Residencies or the Women Make Music fund. Details of the current funds can be found on the PRSF website.

HOW TO APPLY FOR GRANTS: AN EXAMPLE USING GRANTS FOR THE ARTS

Here are some examples of cases for funding that applicants might make.

Case 1: An artist wants to play a concert – for example, he or she has a venue and an audience, but would need a grant to cover the costs involved in putting the concert on including paying musicians, rehearsal costs and marketing. Potential income would come from ticket sales, but there's likely to be a small shortfall. A grant would make all the difference between the concert going ahead or not.

Case 2: An artist is already able to tour commercially with a small band, but wants to produce a larger show in collaboration with another artist and using more musicians. A grant would subsidise the cost of the special expanded show, allowing the production to go ahead.

Case 3: An artist has written a number of songs, and wants to produce an EP and stage a small showcase in order to project the work more widely. A small budget is needed to pay the producer and the musicians involved.

As can be seen, touring and recording can be included within an application to an arts council or similar organisation. That is not to say that grants can be used to subsidise all of the costs of touring or recording, but they can be awarded to musicians who are operating on a not-for-profit or charitable basis.

Once you have the idea, you will need to apply and provide a budget. Grant-funded projects are not supposed to set out to make a profit, and the assessors of the GtfA application will expect to see all of the income and costs related to the project, including income 'in kind' and the ways in which their grant will make a contribution to the project breaking even. The following example is for Case 1 above.

Notice that the artist will be paying him/herself some money. Costs include paying for the musicians (themselves included) and the project management (self-organised). Also notice that the venue hire, which is worth £1,000, is being donated as a form of sponsorship and is listed on both sides of the budget. The reason for including this is to show the 'true cost' of the event, and demonstrate that the grant is paying for a quarter of the costs and not a third of the costs.

Once your funding application has been accepted, you will normally receive an offer letter or contract. This will set out the amount that you are being offered (which may be less than you requested), an agreement for you to sign, and a timetable for the funding. Your timetable should include dates for payments, interim reports (if applicable) and final evaluation of your project.

An interim report will normally be requested where there is a significant sum of money being granted and/or the project is to be carried out over a period of several months, and where the funder wishes to manage the financial risk of the project. In such cases, a funder may stagger payments, giving you some money up front, and further instalments as you progress through the project. Before releasing a second payment, they will ask for an interim report, which sets out how much of the money has already been spent against the budget, what activity has already taken place, how that went, and an explanation of any changes or delays that have occurred. A satisfactory interim report will allow the next payment to be released.

Sample Budget

ITEM	AMOUNT	NOTE
INCOME		
Ticket Sales	£2,000	200 tickets @ £10 each, being 80% of capacity of 250.
ACE Grant	£1,000	Amount of grant subsidy you are applying for, 25% of total costs.
Venue Sponsorship	£1,000	The venue costs £500 to hire plus a sound engineer and equipment costs an additional £500. Due to your longstanding relationship the venue is going to give you this for free. This 'in kind' funding is included in this budget, although some funds ask for it to be shown separately.
TOTAL INCOME	£4,000	
EXPENSES		
Sales and Marketing	£500	Promoting and advertising the concert, designing a flyer, putting out a press release.
Rehearsal Space	£250	Cost of rehearsal space for 2 days.
Musicians' Fees	£2,000	Paying 8 musicians £250 each for rehearsal and performance, including the musician who is applying for the grant.
Project Co-ordination	£250	Paying someone to organise the gig, rehearsal and liaise with the venue.
Venue and Production	£1,000	Equal to the 'venue sponsorship' above, this reflects the actual cost of the venue hire, engineer fee and equipment hire.
TOTAL EXPENSES	£4,000	Income = expenses, this is a balanced budget including the grant subsidy.

Figure 1: Sample Budget

At the end of the project, funders will typically ask for an evaluation. This will be more substantial than an interim report, and could be anything from 500 to 50,000 words depending on the policy of the funder and the scale of the project. The evaluation will ask for the final accounts of the project, and a lot more detail about how it went, the outcomes and any lessons learned or unexpected successes or problems that arose as a result of the work.

If the project is particularly large, there may be a requirement to have an independent evaluation carried out by an external evaluator. Some funders permit you to include an amount in your budget for the cost of an internal or external evaluation, and for the actual costs of accounting, so if the funder requires this, make sure to clarify this point when making your application, otherwise the costs will be passed on to you or your organisation. The final payment will often be withheld until the evaluation is accepted.

REPORTING AND EVALUATION

How Your Application Will Be Assessed: Example From PRSF

The PRSF has some of the best success rates you are likely to get from a charitable foundation, but still only 33 per cent of projects go through the first round of their application process, and just 16 per cent of all applications actually receive some money. One-off programmes like 'New Music 20x12' are even more competitive, because there are a fixed number of awards (20 in that case).

The application process is carefully organised. At stage one, applicants submit a short amount of information and some music.

James Hannam, Grants Manager at PRSF says:

> "Every application requires two external assessors and one member of staff, and no one sees the other's scores, so it's as unbiased as we can make it".

If the music is felt to be of a good standard by the assessors and meets the eligibility criteria, applicants will be invited to apply for the second round. If not, the application will be rejected, but with a minimal amount of time having been invested by applicants and assessors.

PRSF offers support for applicants who make it through to the second round. Few appear to take advantage of it, however, as James Hannam says,

> "At stage two we offer full email and phone support and we get very few enquiries. We actually say on the 'welcome to stage two' email, 'do call us, you're welcome to ask for advice', and still the take up's quite low."

For PRSF applications at stage two you have to provide a budget, a full programme, a marketing plan and a statement from someone you're working with (to demonstrate that your project isn't too 'insular').

According to James Hannam the marketing plan is often a struggle for applicants. He says,

> "A lot of people fall down on the marketing plan, that's the weakest point of nearly every application, because we really want to know that what we fund will be seen by a decent audience."

Hannam suggests going beyond relying on your existing friends and family audience, and social media – most of the marketing plans he receives are identical in this respect. Therefore doing things in imaginative new ways is encouraged. For example, applicants could engage with a particular community, society, interest group or audience in an innovative way that will attract a new audience and ensure that people know about the project.

Another weak point can be the budget. As detailed in the Grants for the Arts section previously, with grants, the funder will always want to see the money coming in and the money going out balance. If your project costs £1,000, the grant plus other income generated must also equal £1,000. Even if there are additional sources of income or costs in the final analysis, you can't apply for money you are not going to spend, or show lots of activity that isn't covered by the grant, without demonstrating how the additional money will be raised. James Hannam explains:

> "A lot of people ask 'if I make a profit will I be penalised?' and the answer's no. We want people to be successful. But for the purposes of this project and application, as it's presented to us, [income and expenditure] have to match."

This principle is essential for grant funding, and can confuse applicants because it is so different from a profit-focused budget for a business plan.

TIPS FROM FUNDING OFFICERS ON GETTING GRANT FUNDING

1. Read the question

Funders complain that applicants often fail to read and answer the question. These applicants write what they want to write rather than what the funder needs to know.

2. Check Eligibility

Make sure you are eligible for the funding you are applying for, and that you meet the criteria of the funder. Not being eligible is the main reason that the majority of applications fall at the first hurdle. Criteria will usually be published; check if you are not sure.

3. Provide Evidence

Provide evidence that you are good at what you do. If you are asked to submit music or video, make sure that it is your best work and is as well-recorded and clear as possible.

4. Write Enough

It doesn't need to be a tome, but if the word limit is 300 words, a few sentences will not suffice. It looks like you don't care, and the assessor will not want to give you a grant.

5. Proofread

Make sure your spelling is correct and the application is easy to read. Assessors are likely to be unsympathetic towards poorly presented applications. If you can't be bothered to take care over your application it gives the impression you are not likely to be very careful in spending and accounting for the funder's grant money either.

6. Be well organised

You need to show who will be running the project, where it will be taking place, who will be taking part, who will be delivering the work and what the outcomes will be.

7. Be Original

Show evidence that you're offering something distinctive. If you're doing something that is unoriginal, how inspiring to the funder is your work likely to be? Funders are often interested in work that is developing the art form, offers a new collaboration or creates some other new work.

8. Think about marketing

How are audiences going to find out about your work and experience it? How would grant funding help you to achieve your plans in this respect?

9. Match-Fund if appropriate

Bear in mind that you can apply for more than one grant. In fact it may be that you are more likely to get funding if you already have a commitment from another funder – PRS funding is sometimes seen as a 'stamp of musical quality' in which other funders have confidence, or local authority funding can help when applying to ACE because it demonstrates acknowledged local need.

10. Get your timing right

There are opening and closing dates for some funds, which you must meet, and also a turnaround time that you will need to be aware of. There's no point in applying to a fund with a six-week decision-making period for an event in five weeks time. You will be rejected. Check if decisions are made after a given closing date, or as applications are received. An early application could be beneficial where other applicants have left theirs to the last minute.

KEY MUSIC GRANT GIVING ORGANISATIONS

Presented in no particular order, I consider the following list of leading organisations to be priority-funding destinations for many projects. Their prominence and popularity means that they are all highly specific in terms of their eligibility, application and funding criteria. An extensive list of additional trusts and foundations that fund music can be found in the Additional Trusts and Foundations section of this book.

EMI Music Sound Foundation

The EMI Music Sound Foundation provides two types of awards: the Instrument and/or Equipment awards allow schools, music teachers and individuals in full-time education to apply directly to the Foundation for assistance with the purchase of musical instruments and/or equipment. There are also bursary awards, which allow students at specific partner colleges to apply for assistance with fees and/or living expenses.

BRIT Trust

The BRIT Trust provides funding for young people in music education, with the BRIT School for Performing Arts in Croydon and Nordoff Robbins Music Therapy regularly receiving support. It also supports charities helping children internationally. Its 2013 charity is War Child. The Trust only considers applications from organisations with charitable status in the UK, and not individuals. It will fund projects, but not capital grants for building or large purchases. Applications are considered once a year in September, and the trust asks that applications are submitted via its website no later than August for projects planned for the following year.

Other organisations funded include Music4Good, Heart 'N' Soul, Chicken Shed, Roundhouse Trust, Mencap, Music and the Deaf, Musicians' Benevolent Fund, Drugscope, and Young Voices.

Musicians' Benevolent Fund Emerging Excellence Award[6]

The MBF [N.B. now called Help Musicians UK] helps musicians in need of financial welfare, for example, if they become ill. However it also has an Emerging Excellence Award to support promising young musicians aged 18–30 who are completing their training and at the beginning of their professional careers.

The projects the Award can support include short specialised courses, coaching or a creative residency or collaborations with other artists.

The project should be related to a clear plan for improving artistic and career development.

The MBF says: "Innovative proposals and those demonstrating a high level of entrepreneurialism are particularly encouraged." It has two tiers of support – smaller grants of £500 – £1,500 and grants of over £1,500. The maximum is £3,000.

There are a few rounds of applications each year, and applicants have to complete an online form and provide a referee. If they are shortlisted, and their grant request is for over £1,500, they would have to pitch to a panel of people.

The Fund also makes individual awards and prizes to music students and young professionals, and may make contributions to musicians' healthcare costs and other small awards.

European Culture Fund

The programme of the EU Culture Fund closed in 2012. However in the new EU budget there will be money available from 2014 onwards for something called 'Creative Europe'. This will hopefully see a 37 per cent increase in funding for culture, and a fusing of the culture and media strategies of the commission. Cultural organisations in Europe will be able to apply, and the funding should be announced in late 2013. It will include some money for a financial guarantee facility (loan guarantees), managed by the European Investment Fund.

The Jerwood Charitable Foundation

The Jerwood Charitable Foundation supports individual artists and organisations through its small grants programme. Its core focus is on the professional development of artists and the exploration of artistic ideas.

However it is highly selective about who it supports. The Foundation states:

"The majority of our partnerships and initiatives are proactively sought and developed, however we do accept unsolicited proposals. Please note [their emphasis] that we very rarely fund projects which are put forward in this way and are seeking specific, targeted, tangible professional development opportunities in the work that we take on."

Some of its recent support for music has gone to partners such as Aldeburgh Music, Aurora Orchestra, Glyndebourne, The Opera Group, Take Five (Jazz, Serious) and PRS for Music Foundation 20x12.

Applicants are required to send a short two-page proposal and budget in the first round, and applications can be made throughout the year.

European Regional Development Fund

•Supporting economic growth through managing the European Regional Development Fund

•ERDF National Guidance

•Generator

Detailed information about ERDF funds are included here because although it is a highly complex scheme, a large number of music companies have benefited from its funds, and the industry would do well to try to understand it better.

ERDF is EU funding that is targeted at areas that need to improve their 'economic competitiveness', meaning creating new jobs and improving businesses. The funding is managed by the Department for Communities and Local Government (DCLG) and has been running since 1975. This is significant funding, for which you would need to be an organisation or a business to apply for.

Over the life of the current ERDF programme (2007–13) London has received £181.9 million of funding, while the North West region has received £755.5 million as it was considered to be in greater need of regeneration. Each region will have its own priorities, but most will include job creation and retention as one of their aims, and over the last decade there has been a strategy of funding IP and the creative and knowledge economy, particularly in regions that have previously been dominated by heavy industry. This has created the rationale to develop programmes that provide training and help for people who want to start a business or develop their skills in music.

Organisations can apply for programmes that meet ERDF priorities. They need matched funding typically meaning 50 per cent of the funding must come from another source. For example, Generator, the Music Development Agency in the North East of England, matches ERDF funding with Arts Council England funding, meaning that they are able to devise projects that achieve both ERDF and Arts Council England goals, yet neither funder bears all the cost and risk. There are three priority objectives in that region at present; the most relevant is regional competitiveness and employment.

Jo Thornton, Director of Resources at Generator, is an expert on funding, and told me that there are changes coming to the ERDF. She explained that there are on-going EU level negotiations for the 2014–2020 ERDF programme, currently, and that there will almost certainly be less money made available. Therefore, there will be competition between nations and regions to win funding, and projects might be expected to be more international with funding to the UK possibly reduced.

The UK coalition Government has created a system of Local Enterprise Partnerships (LEPs) that replace the old Regional Development Agencies (RDAs). In future LEPs will largely be responsible for bidding for ERDF funding in their local area, so the local priorities will be decided by these groups; and creative industries and IP may or may not be on their agenda.

There are certain programmes that SMEs can apply for. The process is highly bureaucratic; the North West Regional ERDF strategy, for example, is over 200 pages long. The way to apply is to keep an eye out locally and nationally for funds and priorities being announced. Usually there will be a call for proposals (there may be several rounds), for which you would have to submit your plans, supporting letters, details of partners you plan to work with and so on. There are some business-specific funds created using ERDF money, and this also occurs at a local level. In the current programme, for example, the East Midlands has a loan fund for businesses, and the East of England region has a VC fund operated by the University of East Anglia.

You can track the money by starting with the national government websites, and tracking its flow to your area. A list of beneficiaries is usually published, providing a useful checklist for your area, detailing where the money has been allocated. Universities, BIS services, development agencies, councils, business parks, charities and other business services have all won funding of between £1,000 and £5 million for projects to support development.

NESTA

Nesta is an independent charity and leading investor in innovation in the UK. It provides investments and grants across a range of funding schemes but key focus is young innovative businesses, creatives and social enterprises.

A typical example of its funding schemes is the Digital R&D Fund, the purpose of which is to maximise audience engagement in the arts, and a total of £7 million has been made available for projects during the period 2012–15 with a maximum of £125,000 awarded per successful applicant (though the majority of projects are considerably below this threshold).

It's important to note that this is not a music- specific fund, and a university research partner is one of several key criteria.

. . .

Paul Hamlyn Foundation

The Paul Hamlyn Foundation is one of the larger independent grant-making foundations in the UK. Its main focus is related to children, young people, and those deemed to be disadvantaged. However, it is open minded and interested in new thinking and important unexplored opportunities.

The author's analysis of the data highlights that in 2012 the Paul Hamlyn Foundation awarded a total of £4,257,347 to its arts programme scheme. Of this £717,500 was given to specific music related projects. Awards were between £10,000 and £120,000. Dividing the total fund between the numbers of recipients shows the average award to be £55,200.

Royal Philharmonic Society

The Royal Philharmonic Society concentrates most of its efforts on the future of classical music. It supports and works with talented young performers and composers under the guise of championing excellence and encouraging, developing and sustaining audiences.

In 2012 it awarded a total of £166,148 to the classical music sector of the industry, with awards ranging between £1,000 and £23,850 depending on the specific fund/grant/scholarship/prize/bursary.

It is important to note that for every fund/grant/prize it awards, specific criteria apply and its overriding focus is classical music.

Calouste Gulbenkian Foundation

The Calouste Gulbenkian Foundation, whose headquarters are in Portugal, is a charitable foundation with cultural, educational, social and scientific interests. The primary aim of the UK branch is to help bring about long-term improvements in wellbeing by fostering connections across boundaries (national, of sector, social, etc.), with a special interest in supporting those who are most disadvantaged. It is important to understand that music and the arts are not their main focus, but it does fund a number of schemes each year.

My investigation into the UK branch's annual reports highlights that, in 2012, the total pot allocated to the arts (in general) was £418,500. Out of this funding pot, £145,000 was awarded to music-related projects under their 'Participatory Performing Arts' strand of their 'Cultural Understanding' programme, which focuses on grassroots artistic initiatives.

The strand is currently organised under the aim of 'Maximising Social and Cultural Value', however, a process of redesign of the Foundation's strategic aims will lead to this strand being managed under the aegis of the Cultural Understanding Programme.

UK Trade & Investment (UKTI)

UKTI is part of the government's Department of Business, Innovation and Skills (BIS) that works with UK-based businesses to help them grow their international markets (and encourages international businesses to invest in the UK). It has a number of programmes developed in partnership with music industry trade bodies, that are relevant to music companies and artists wanting to grow their international sales. This includes a range of specialist sectors such as Jazz Music and Musical Instrument Makers, as well as recorded music, music publishing, management and performing artists.

Its Trade Access Programme (TAP) provides financial support for music trade bodies, Accredited Trade Organisations and SMEs to exhibit at overseas trade fairs and funds promotional activity to enhance UK exhibitor groups at those events. TAP is open to companies who are 'solo participants' in music trade events. The programme subsidises the cost to music companies of participating in trade fairs and trade missions.

Through international trade advisers in 40 offices around the UK, and connections with British chambers of commerce and embassies worldwide, it can offer advice, training (such as the Passport to Export Programme) and introductions to local music businesses that will help companies export and develop overseas markets.

UKTI has recently announced The Music Export Growth Scheme. Administered by the BPI it will allocate grants totalling £3 million over three years from September 2013. Open to independent music companies, grants ranging between £5,000–£50,000, will help support international marketing, touring and showcasing. Awards will be made four times a year, following the presentation of detailed campaign proposals to a selection board of industry experts.

FOUR

Friends and Family

Raising money from friends and family is one of the most common ways to seed fund a small business or music career. Beginning with Sofia Hagberg's End Of The Road festival (case study C below), this chapter considers the advantages and pitfalls of raising money from those closest to you. It looks at how to go about asking for money, and includes suggestions of measures you can take to both structure the funding and safeguard relationships, both personal and financial.

———

CASE STUDY C: END OF THE ROAD FESTIVAL

Sofia Hagberg moved to London from Sweden in 1998, and made the most of the city's thriving music culture at the time, regularly going out to clubs and gigs. She quickly made friends with Simon Taffe, another young music fan. By 2005, Taffe was running a decorating business, while Hagberg was working as an Executive PA.

One day Taffe rang Hagberg with the idea of starting a music festival, and she jumped at the chance. She says:

> "I'd always wanted to work in music, but the opportunity for the right kind of job never came along and to organise our own festival was a dream job to me. I had been going to a lot of concerts over the years, and by doing so I had built up a network of friends who worked in music… all of them were saying it would be impossible."

Hagberg, however, was not so sceptical. She had what she describes as "a ton of belief in our vision and ability to make it happen" and was hugely enthusiastic about the idea. Together with Taffe, she became a co-founder of the End of The Road Festival. A third founder also joined the team at this early stage, Philip Wicks, Taffe's bookkeeper, who not only managed the finances of the festival, but also provided a mature and professional face for the company which reassured the venue owners and the licensing authorities as to the seriousness of the project.

Taffe and Hagberg's initial conversation began a gruelling six-month period of work during evenings and weekends to get the idea off the ground. Taffe continued with his decorating business, using its profits to fund the expenses of the festival. In February 2006, the partners agreed that, with the first festival due to take place in September of that year, one of them had to start working on the project full-time, so Hagberg resigned from her day-job. They also quickly realised that they had underestimated the costs of operating the festival, and that they would need to raise a lot of cash in order to deliver it.

As a new business with no track record, like many start-ups, the founders used both their own money and that of friends and family to stage the first festival. Hagberg took out a personal bank loan, Wicks invested some of his personal savings and Taffe had been in the process of selling his house, so when it finally sold he put the proceeds into the business and moved himself and his young family into a rented home. Following this, the festival also received amounts from £5,000 to upwards of £60,000 from family members and friends.

I asked Hagberg how she and Taffe presented their requests for funding. She remembers:

> "We were just asking everyone 'can you help us?' as friends. We believed in the Festival's potential to have a long life".

There were a few reasons why their financial supporters felt comfortable enough to fund what was, on paper, a very risky proposal. First, the founders had a clear vision about what they wanted to achieve, and were very passionate in the way they communicated that dream. To backup their pitch, they developed a document explaining their ethos, listing the 50 bands that would form their dream line-up, and describing in detail how the Festival would look and feel. Second, both of the founders demonstrated their own commitment by putting in huge amounts of their own money and time, and giving people who knew them well the confidence that they would see the project through. Third, Taffe personally guaranteed to repay much of the money even if the Festival failed, which was a huge personal risk.

Hagberg says:

> "it was very scary for Simon as he was the person that took the most risk; he would have to repay all the money if everything failed."

Interestingly, she says that although their bookkeeper had prepared financial information, they didn't actually show their supporters and potential funders any formal budgets or cash flow forecasts. The decision on whether to fund them was really based on the funders' relationships with the founders, their firm belief in the idea and their trust that the money would, eventually, be repaid.

This faith was eventually borne out. In the first year (2006), the Festival sold just 1,600 of its 5,000 capacity, and the company made a loss of around £300,000. In the second year, ticket sales more than doubled to 4,200 tickets, but the company still made a loss of around £100,000[1]. By year three, the Festival had sold out and broken-even. It took at least three to four more years of sold-out festivals before all of the loans were repaid. Today, the capacity has risen to 10,000 people and the Festival makes a healthy profit. It won the Best Small Festival award at the 2011 UK Festival Awards, and has become a firm fixture in the festival calendar. None of this would have been possible without the support of family and friends.

However, when Hagberg described Taffe's and her relationships with some of the funders in more detail, it became clear that arrangements had been reached in an ad-hoc way. Each time the founders received money, they discussed the terms with their funders and exchanged emails with them as a way of recording those discussions in writing. But there were occasions where, due to a lack of formal contract, people had slightly different interpretations of what the agreements were, causing some friction.

In retrospect, Hagberg agrees that these arrangements could and should have been made clearer. She says:

> "Clarity is important as a project like this can be very emotional
> for everyone involved, and people's feelings can change as things

develop. If the project isn't successful, yet they get their money back – they are likely to feel happy and relieved. But if the project is very successful, then maybe someone who's happy to help out for free in the early stages will later wish that they had asked for interest or for a share of the ownership or similar. At times like this, a clear agreement is invaluable as, otherwise, you may be putting family ties and friendships at risk."

Asked if her founders had put repayment agreements in place with their friends and family, she said that that the lenders were very patient and the arrangements were informal. No one charged interest on their loan, and when repayments first started, they were made irregularly. Later on, lenders would ask them to repay some of the money as and when they needed it back, and repayments became more regular and formalised over time. Hagberg says that after the first Festival, they put early-bird tickets for the following year on sale immediately. This generated cash in advance, which helped ease the pressure on the company to fund the event by borrowing money. By selling the tickets directly themselves rather than using a ticket agent, they were able to draw from these funds as soon as the money came in.

TIPS ON FRIENDS AND FAMILY FUNDING

1. Ask for help

Don't be afraid to ask for help, your friends and family can be great supporters of your business.

2. Show what you're putting in

Demonstrate your own commitment to the project as strongly as you can, which might require putting in some of your own money, as well as lots of time and effort.

3. Evidence your plan

Be prepared to back your idea up with written plans and financial information, and to answer questions.

4. Consider what's in it for them

Work out the limits of what you are willing to give up in return for funding.

5. Consider future scenarios

If you are unsuccessful, just break even or are very successful, how will you divide up the company and its liabilities, and how would this affect each individual founder, lender or investor?

6. Get it in writing

Make formal agreements to keep the business and personal relationships clearly defined. You might not feel this is necessary at the time, but it can prove critical if things don't go to plan, or if you achieve unexpected success.

WHY IS FRIENDS AND FAMILY IMPORTANT FOR A BOOK ON FUNDING?

Funding for small music businesses has been shown by researchers to come from similar sources as those for other small businesses. Indeed, using your own money (bootstrapping) or money lent, gifted or invested by your family and friends is the most common way of funding a small business. The Federation of Small Businesses says that 35 per cent of members who have been trading for one to two years have used money from friends and family as a way of financing their business in the last 12 months[2]. They suggest that with micro-businesses and new start-ups the figures would be higher.

In fact, it is such a widespread occurrence that it is described in business books as the three F's – friends, family and fools. If the 'fools' tag sounds a bit worrying, then it should be. It indicates that at the early and small stages, most businesses are so uncertain of success that the risks of putting money in are extremely high. On the positive side, those who know you well are likely to be the most sympathetic funders, have goals very closely aligned to your own, and of course are able to offset the risk by knowing your track record and having more insight than a non-related lender or investor into what your abilities and chances of success are.

Investment expert Davin McDermott of management consultancy Createch Consulting says that he is seeing "more and more" friends and family deals among the music and media companies he advises. I spoke to Berkley Edwards, a solicitor at Clintons, who also says that he is seeing quite a few friends and family private deals with artists. I asked him what sort of money his clients typically raised. Edwards says:

> "It depends on so many factors, but I've seen a number of artists raise five or ten thousand pounds to record an album and get some equipment together. Equally I've seen artists take £100,000 pounds from a private investor."

So these private deals can be substantial. I will look at the implications of receiving them in the form of gifts, loans or investment.

1. Gifts

If you have friends and family who are willing and able to give you gifts, that can be a wonderful boost to your project. This support may be 'in kind' (paying for equipment, providing you with accommodation, transportation or studio space), or in cash. This is the simplest of the three ways that they can help you. However if you receive cash gifts, it may be worthwhile establishing a paper trail as evidence that the money is a gift.

Ensure that you are on the same page as the person giving you the money, and that they are not expecting to be repaid (either as a loan, or sometime in the future if you make it big). You could do this verbally, or even better let them know that you want to confirm that it is a gift when you write them your thank you letter or email.

Be aware that if the donor of the gift were to have enough assets upon their death to put them over the threshold for Inheritance Tax (IHT), then cash gifts they made in the seven years before their death would be liable to IHT, paid for by the giver's estate. The gift could still be exempt from IHT, even under these circumstances, because individuals can make as many small gifts of under £250 as they wish in a tax year, and a gift of up to £3,000 to one person. IHT is only likely to be of concern if they are making a large gift of thousands of pounds, but if this is the case they may be wealthy enough to establish that they are making a gift out of surplus income (not savings) which is another way to exempt the gift from IHT.

Recipients do not have to pay income tax on a cash gift; so in case of an inspection of your tax affairs, you may want to have a record that it is a gift and not payment for any services.

One of the advantages of a gift is of course that you do not have to repay it. Provided that it is clear to both parties that it will be a gift, the giver can afford it, and that you are both aware of the tax issues that can arise, this is one of the simplest ways of getting funding. Be sensitive about your relationship with the giver. Although they are making a gift, the giver will probably want to know what you have done with the money and how it has benefitted you, so remember to thank them and report back on how things have gone. Be aware that they may feel that their gift entitles them to comment or advise on how you run your business or career, so be prepared to thank them graciously for their advice!

2. Loans

A loan from a friend or family member needs to be treated with caution. The most important thing is to ask them if they can afford to lose the money, in the worst case scenario. If this loss would cause them hardship, suggest that they get some independent advice on this, or do not accept the loan. Berkeley Edwards, of law firm Clintons says: "The moment you're asking anyone to give more money than they're comfortable with, the obligation to keep them happy becomes almost overwhelming."

If they can afford to take a risk, then you need to consider what your repayment terms will be.

The first thing to consider is: will they charge interest? If they do, then that provides them with a small interest income, which they will have to declare to HMRC.

Second, the loan would form part of their estate. In the event of their death, would it be repayable in full or written off? What would happen if one of the parties dies or is out of work, or the lender needs the money back?

Third, will it be paid in a lump sum or in stages? Will there be any agreement that payments can slip if there are cash flow problems? The flexible payment terms, no arrangement fees and lower interest rates that friends and family typically offer can be a great advantage to your small business or music career.

What will the amount of the repayments be and when will they be timed? You could link repayments to your cash flow; when you get money in, the funder gets a percentage of that until the cash is repaid.

Finally, what will the funder's input be on the business? Will they have the right to see accounts and have input into the business (which could be useful if they have financial or business knowledge)? Will you be reporting to them on a regular basis, or will they have no say once they have made the loan? Are you allowed to spend the loan money freely, without checking on the exact use with them?

Again, it is good to exchange letters and/or emails setting this out, and if the amount is substantial, consider paying a small fee to have an agreement drawn up by a solicitor. If both the lender and the borrower are clear about what they are entering into, then this can avoid resentment or misunderstandings between you.

Berkeley Edwards recommends a simple contract, because often friends and family are not going to go and get their own separate legal advice. He says, "it can be very user-friendly - you give us £500 and in return we will give you this benefit - designed for non-lawyers to read."

The advantages of a loan from friends and family are that it should be lower cost and more flexible than a commercial loan, and almost certainly easier to obtain. The borrower may pay no interest, or a lower rate of interest on a loan from their family than they would do from a bank. A disadvantage is that often, family members aren't fully aware of the risks of losing their money, the loan will normally be treated as personal to you, and if your relationship with the lender continues but the business fails, you might still be expected to pay it back. Make sure that it is very clear to the lender how the loan will be structured, what you will be using it for, and what will happen if things go wrong.

In terms of your relationship with the lender, as long as things are going well and they get their money back, then they are unlikely to be concerned. However if you fail to make a payment, you might find they want more of a say in what you are doing, and have a view about your personal financial affairs. If you fall on hard times and make an effort to put in place a repayment plan, lenders are more likely to be sympathetic, but if they see you spending money when you still owe loan payments to them, the relationship could easily be damaged.

3. Investment

Investment is a more complicated way to structure money from friends and family, but it has the advantage of being more attractive for the investor because if your business does really well, they could stand to profit from your success. Also, there are ways of structuring an investment so that the friend or family member can benefit from tax reliefs for investors. This can help reduce the risk to them of losing their investment, and if they do lose their money they will be able to offset those losses against other income. The value of the deal will dictate the complexity of it: for small amounts of money it probably is not worth paying for the costs of setting up a complex tax structure. If the investment is sizeable, perhaps tens of thousands of pounds, then it can be worthwhile taking professional advice.

Berkeley Edwards described deals whereby an artist creates a business around a specific project such as an album and tour, and offers a share of profits to an investor. First the artist has to decide what income they are going to include in the deal – for example, recording sales, performance royalties, live income, publishing income, synch income, merchandise, sponsorship. When the money comes in, 50 per cent is allocated to the artist and 50 per cent to the investors until they have recouped their investment, at which point the investor's percentage of the profits reduces. Once the investor has recouped an agreed amount, say, two or three times their original investment, either their right to a share will end, or will continue at a very low level on an on-going basis, just for that specific project.

A similar model that Edwards has used with single private investors, is one in which, in return for a sum of money, the investor would participate in all of the income streams of the artist. A deal would be set up whereby the investor would receive a percentage of net income (income after the expenses of producing recordings and other costs have been taken into account) until they had recouped their investment. The investor would then earn a lower percentage of net income, but only for a fixed time period.

Of course the way the deal is structured also depends on the tax implications for the investor. If the investor is looking to take advantage of tax relief for investors who put money into start-up businesses, they may want the business to qualify for the Seed Enterprise Investment Scheme (SEIS). This is a set of tax rules that give investors 50 per cent tax relief on their investment in qualifying companies (i.e. 50 per cent of what they invest can be deducted from their income tax bill). There is a cost and complexity to getting approval to use SEIS as a company, and your company will have to pay for professional advice on this. There is more detail on SEIS in the Investment chapter of this book.

There are also a couple of exclusions relating to money from friends and family. Certain people are treated as associates for the purposes of SEIS, and together the associates cannot own more than 30 per cent of the shares in the qualifying SEIS company between them. 'Associates' include business partners, spouses and civil partners, parents and grandparents, children and grandchildren. Brothers and sisters are not counted as associates for SEIS purposes. And of course neither are friends, provided you are not already financially linked with them.

The advantages of investment are that it may be more suitable than a loan if you are looking to hold onto the money in the long term, and have a plan for growth. Investors are likely to be more patient than lenders, and might be willing to wait for a few years before they see any return. They will get a share of your success, so their goals will be aligned with yours in the long term. The tax advantages for investors of large amounts of money can be a great incentive. Of course, if you don't make any money, you will not have to repay the investment.

A disadvantage could be the complexity of such investments, particularly if the business needs to qualify for SEIS or its big brother, the Enterprise Investment Scheme (EIS). Investors are likely to expect to be much more involved and get much more information from you in terms of reporting; it is not uncommon for them to ask to see management accounts or to be a director in the company.

Business Consultant Davin McDermott of Create Tech sounds a note of caution:

> "I think that friends or family and money should not mix, because it's a recipe for disaster. As it's friends and family, people sometimes forget that you still need structures there, you need to have objectivity, and the time to put it in place is at the beginning when everyone is very excited and in the honeymoon period."

Still, McDermott admits that he once invested in a family member's company (things didn't work out), and that it is natural that one's vision will be clouded when it comes to one's friends and family. All investments carry some level of risk and people shouldn't invest their money unless they can afford to lose it. Make sure you don't reach the point where you have irresponsibly blown your parents' life savings: facing them at family gatherings would become pretty difficult!

TIPS ON GETTING INVESTMENT FROM FRIENDS AND FAMILY

1. Make a plan

You may be very comfortable approaching friends and family for money, but it is still worthwhile giving them as much information as possible. This is especially important if you are going to try to raise large amounts of investment, in which case you should prepare a full business plan. In the case of smaller scale investments, a business plan shows that you have done your research and planning, and are taking the investor's financial commitment seriously. However small the amount, you should consider taking the time to write a short business plan, even if it is only one or two pages. It should include what you plan to do, what the funder is putting in, what they're getting in return, a sales forecast and a break-even point. Treat it as formally as you can.

2. Make a proper presentation

Warn your friend or family member that you want to make them a proposal, and set a time to do this. Explain in detail what you want to do, what type of funding you want, and how much you need. Allow them to ask questions, give them time to consider their response, and be polite if they decline.

3. Leverage

Consider combining your friends and family money with a crowdfunding campaign to reach a wider group of family and friends who you would find it too awkward or time consuming to pitch to directly.

4. Report Back

Be clear about how you will report back to them. Will you email them at regular intervals to let them know how things are going? Will you discuss it over the dinner table, or will you have formal meetings? Do not leave it for them to chase you for updates. Be proactive.

How will the decisions be made? Will they be consulted on how money is spent, and will they get financial reports?

How will they get their money back? If the money is an investment or a loan, there are a flexible number of ways to structure this.

What if your circumstances change? Will they be able to ask for the loan back and what if you can no longer work on the project, or the project fails?

Ultimately, funding from friends and family has been an important part of the financing of many musicians and music businesses. However, treating this funding source too casually can lead to damaging misunderstandings; a frank discussion about some of the different scenarios that might arise and putting something in writing will help protect both your business and personal relationships.

FIVE

Crowdfunding

Tom Williams and The Boat (case study D below) and James Yuill (case study E below) detail two successful crowdfunding campaigns and explore the challenges faced by these artists. This chapter will then look at the different forms crowdfunding can take and profile three of the most important sites for crowdfunded music. It concludes with some useful tips and a list of alternative sites you could use.

———

CASE STUDY D: TOM WILLIAMS AND THE BOAT

Tom Williams was a solo singer-songwriter, playing gigs around Kent, when he met the other five members of what became Tom Williams and The Boat. The band formed in 2007, and by 2008 had started getting radio play through BBC Introducing[1], which led to an opportunity for a radio session. It was while the group were recording this at the BBC's Maida Vale studios that they met producer Simon Askew.

The Boat self-financed their first album, partly using income from their performance royalties and support from Simon and other professionals who did work on a free, commission or contingency basis. By the time of the second album, *Teenage Blood*, the band were being managed by independent label Moshi Moshi, which suggested The Boat consider crowdfunding their album through a Pledge Music campaign[2].

SETTING UP AND RUNNING THE CAMPAIGN

Williams does not think the financial vehicle of getting people to pay in advance is particularly revolutionary, but explains that Pledge Music encourages you to:

> "Take the fans on a journey through the project, and… make an enormous effort to talk to them and update them on how the project's going. The biggest thing that Pledge gets artists to do is treat their audience better."

Some costs were covered by the band's management, but the cost of producing the album and fulfilling the pledges was borne by the band's own label.

It took Tom Williams two to three hours per day over four months to raise £6,000, which was spent as follows:

£900 (15 per cent Pledge Music commission)

£255 (5 per cent post Pledge Music commission to Kent Air Ambulance)[3]

£3,145 costs of making, packing and posting pledges and other fulfilment costs

£1,700 towards the £5,000 cost of producing the album

Williams says he encountered the difficulty of losing momentum in the middle of the campaign:

> "After the initial massive outpouring of support from our fans when we raised £3,000 on the first day, the days after when we raised just £20 a day were the days when I felt like I was flogging it really."

Some of the things he did to sustain his campaign included recording acoustic demos of the songs on the album that would only be available to fans who bought the album through the Pledge campaign, and incrementally adding new offers and updates, as all of the crowdfunding sites recommend. The campaign got a late boost because of the mainstream media when a lead song went to radio and press. Williams explains:

> "[Fans] are all different in the amounts that they want to give, and it's directly proportional to how much you want to give away, too. A fan that you pick up on BBC Radio 1 is typically a much younger person with a shorter attention span and with one eye on trends, and is completely different to the 37-year-old that you pick up on BBC6 Music who pledges £400 for a house party or a house gig. I think it's worth noting that our campaign probably worked because most of our audience came from BBC6 Music whose age demographic is late 20s to early 40s, so it's the mature, well-educated music fan with a disposable income that can commit to that kind of financial burden. A 16-year-old who thinks you're

the best thing she's ever heard really can't afford more than the £8 for a download. So you've got to know your audience."

FULFILLING PLEDGES

Like most bands of this size, the members are not all full time musicians. Band member Ant Vicary is a dairy farmer, for example, so Williams really led the campaign on behalf of the band, and did all the updates. While he enjoyed the contact he had with fans of the band, some of the pre-fulfilment tasks required lots of attention to detail.

> "It's like a constant public relations project, you just get loads and loads of emails from people saying 'I see you've got the blue t-shirt in small but I'm a medium...' and it takes up days..."

Nevertheless, Williams says he did get something out of the customer service element of the campaign:

> "If you're going to cut out the middle man and sell music in your own store online, this is a far more personable way to do it, in that you can have daily interaction with your fans. So it does improve the artist-fan relationship, and they really feel that they brought you through something."

Another challenge for the band was fulfilling all of the pledges. While their CDs were shipped from a warehouse, other items such as framed, handwritten lyrics and posters required special packaging which the band had to buy, pack and ship themselves. Williams laughs ruefully:

"you need to take all these hundreds of things down to your local post office, you forget how much work all that is, that's like a whole couple of days work."

Some of the pledges that worked best were 'write a song with Tom Williams' and 'House gigs', because they were based on offering a special experience for the fan around what the band do best – write songs and play live. William says:

"We did four house parties as part of our pledge campaign... 'Pledgers' might actually be co-writers on the next Tom Williams and the Boat album... the songs from them are really good."

The pledges turned out to be more valuable than just receiving money, as Williams says:

"Those people still email me and say 'hello'... they're part of the bigger family now; it certainly wouldn't have happened if we'd just lobbed a pre-order up on HMV."

TOM WILLIAMS' TIPS FOR A NEW(-ISH) BAND CONSIDERING CROWDFUNDING

1. Get a mailing list

Build up an audience before attempting a crowdfunding project. Using things like an 'email for media' widget is really good – it allows you to give away your best track for free, and put it on the front page of all your website(s), your Facebook page, Twitter and so on in order to build up an email database.

2. Know your audience

Talk to your fans on a regular basis. Really work out what they want. You've got to think quite selflessly as you're asking people for quite a lot of money. You don't have an automatic right to their money, so you have to offer everything that you can to make them happy.

3. Don't expect the campaign to bring in lots of new fans

Williams says that only 5 per cent of their campaign funding was generated by new fans, so it was more about monetising the goodwill that they had from existing fans.

4. Invest the time

Be prepared to invest time and effort into communicating with fans during the campaign.

5. Consider your platform

Weigh up the support you will get with your campaign from the crowdfunding platform you use.

CROWDFUNDING, A WAY OF LIFE?

I asked Williams if the band would be funding their next recording using a crowdfunding platform. He recognised that in some ways, the Pledge Music campaign has become part of the band's identity, in the same way that MySpace was part of the Arctic Monkeys' story, but he was unsure about whether it will continue to be part of what they do:

> "The more people that launch campaigns, the less it's newsworthy: it just becomes something that people do". It was occasionally a struggle: "Fans want to follow your trajectory… doing a similar

project again feels like a bit you're stagnating. I think it would feel less like you're on the right track. It feels a bit like begging sometimes."

Williams also became aware of the risk of pushing the fanbase too far to participate in too many crowdfunding and crowdsourcing campaigns, or indeed boring them. He says:

"I'm not sure I'd feel comfortable doing it again. I think it was an amazing experience and something that we and our fanbase really enjoyed, but I think it's a stepping stone… coming back with a new campaign, we're going to have to do something different."

———————

CASE STUDY E: JAMES YUILL

London-based James Yuill used to source music for adverts, before he decided to develop his part-time singer-songwriter activities into a full time career.

He met his manager Amul Batra of Twinki Management a month later, and his music began to take off. Three albums later and following a two-year hiatus from releasing new music, Batra persuaded Yuill to crowdfund his fourth album.

Although he was already a user of Pledge Music (giving money to other bands), Yuill took a bit of convincing as to whether it was the right vehicle for him. He reveals that he was unsure about contacting fans directly and asking them for money. However, eventually he found that communicating with fans prior to a release through the medium of the crowdfunding campaign was more effective than returning to the market and immediately trying to enter into a record release cycle.

The record *These Spirits* was released on Yuill's own label, something he now feels confident in doing, having worked with an outside label for earlier albums:

> "It's come full circle. I've had so much more freedom and control with this in terms of making all the decisions, I had no idea [with the first release] about the promo thing; that you had to plan all that months before."

PRE-LAUNCH PLANNING

It was, Yuill explains, a long process to develop the campaign and raise the money, and one that he needed help with.

> "I don't think I could have done it without a manager thinking through it all, coming up with all the ideas."

To begin with, the team considered a target amount to raise. They then developed a long list of possible pledges (rewards), and worked out the costs. If it was a physical item, such as selling one of Yuill's guitars for example, they had to consider the cost of postage and packaging to anywhere in the world. Items ended up being sent as far as Japan, Indonesia and Canada. There was also the cost of making or buying the items, such as the 'silly gift a week for one month' pledge (yours for £25) or a handwritten lyric sheet (for £20). Remembering this, he laughs:

> "I did it on a big A3 sheet with felt tip pens, so they could frame them – it took ages, I kept smudging it and having to start again".

There were other items that were free to deliver, such as putting pledgers' names in the credits of the CD, which ultimately proved the most profitable pledge. Yuill cautions:

"You have to make sure each pledge makes you money, they all need to add up to profit overall. Postage is a huge part of it, physically getting everything fulfilled."

To kick off the campaign, Yuill made a pledge video that asked fans to contribute to his campaign. He says:

"My campaign had a hint of comedy. I wanted to use my voice and not a corporate voice. It was me doing all the ideas. That all adds to it; if you can sell yourself and give all of yourself to the pledge campaign. Be yourself. I enjoy the comedic side, so I went for that."

THE CONTENT MACHINE

Yuill raised 25 per cent of his £6,000 target on the first day of the campaign, and 50 per cent in the first week, after which it slowed down considerably. He added around two pieces of original content every week for three months to keep the momentum going. Each one had to be thought through and created by the artist. Whenever he posted these, he could track 'spikes' in the pre-orders, and it was a good structure to use to keep people interested. He made an effort to keep content unique to avoid boring people. The most successful pieces of content were cover versions, a previously unreleased music video and video diaries. The music video was successful because, says Yuill:

> "It had the biggest production values, it was lots of still images used to create a video, and it was the most impactful piece of content."

Video diaries also worked well. He thanked people for pledging, answered questions about how he makes his tracks, showed fans 'virtually' around his studio, and generally interacted with them.

> "Because I'd engaged with people, rather than just sticking a track up, video diaries were the second most impactful piece of content."

Yuill suggests stockpiling content before starting, as he found it time-consuming to generate new ideas while trying to keep everything fresh

> "That was probably the hardest part, keeping people interested and figuring out how I could keep interacting with people and generate sales. It was a good process."

Ultimately, Yuill says:

> "I would definitely do it again. It did monopolise my life for that three months; I think most people don't appreciate how much you have to put into the process."

He advises getting organised, calculating costs very carefully, working out how you will fulfil things within the time limits set by Pledge Music at the end of the campaign, and get as much content prepared as you can before starting the campaign. If you can, get a friend or assistant to help with both ideas and fulfilling mail orders.

CAMPAIGN RESULTS

£6,374 (no VAT – take advice on whether you include this)

£945 (commission at £15 per cent)

£100 (estimated donation to charity)

£500 (cost of pledges)

£4,829 Gross Profit

Overall, Yuill found the experience to be very hard work but he was ultimately successful in raising the necessary funds. Asked if it had changed his relationship with his fans, he said that although he communicates a lot with them on Twitter already, it had been beneficial overall, and a fantastic experience. He was not sure if the campaign had generated any new fans.

He "recognised a lot of the names" and was now very aware of and closer to his hardcore fans.

> "I meet loads of the fans at gigs anyway. The ones further afield are hugely loyal and invested a lot into my campaign. Their name is in your head forever as the ones who put their faith in you. It does give you an insight into who your fans are and the sorts of people they are. It's quite touching to see how much people are willing to invest in you and your album, even though you might not have met them."

WHAT IS CROWDFUNDING?

Crowdfunding is the pooling of small contributions of money from a group of people for the purpose of making something larger happen than would have previously been possible. Most people probably associate crowdfunding with the online platforms that have proliferated and grabbed headlines over the last five years. There are plenty of examples of art and music having been funded by public subscription that precede these digital tools however. In 1824, the members of the Royal Philharmonic Society funded the commission of Beethoven's 9th Symphony. In 1997, rock band Marillion successfully invited fans to contribute thousands of dollars to fund a US tour, proving the concept to the music industry. Shortly after that came the launch of charitable giving and sponsorship sites such as JustGiving (in 2000), which allow the public to give money online, thereby replacing the traditional paper sponsorship form, leveraging the public's increasing comfort with ecommerce. The launch of online crowdfunding platforms that particularly feature music came in the late-noughties, with companies like SellaBand and Slicethepie (2007), Indiegogo (2008), Kickstarter and Pledge Music (2009).

The various online platforms allow you to offer different things to an individual funder in exchange for their money. This chapter focuses on platforms that allow you to collect donations; or exchange donations for rewards. Two other types of crowdfunding platform are referenced in the chapters on investment and debt respectively.

At the time of writing, reward-based crowdfunding platforms are gaining a huge amount of popularity in the music industry. They are aiming to unite the music industry's intimate knowledge of social media marketing, its need to find alternative sources of money to fund artists' careers, and the industry's indie/DIY culture.

There is something appealingly transparent and democratic about the idea of crowdfunding that relies on the creativity and commitment of the artist and support team. The main skills it requires – offering good music, nurturing a fanbase and creating excitement – would be essential for any independent artist to succeed. The time invested in building a crowdfunding campaign is time well spent, as it necessarily deepens artists' relationships with their fanbases and forces them to learn promotional skills that will come in handy later on in their careers. There is also a huge upside to generating income before creating expenditure, namely improved cash flow, something that has always been particularly difficult for artists to manage.

Online crowdfunding has been hyped as the future of the music industry – some sort of magic tonic for a 'grassroots' or 'legacy' artist's career. The simple truth remains; not everyone who aspires to fund a full-time music career will be able to successfully achieve this. Crowdfunding as a process is, by its nature, more democratic than other funding options, and permits artists a level of independence they might not have enjoyed in other circumstances. The problem is that you massively increase the number of people that need convincing to invest in you, as opposed to the 'traditional' label route. This can mean considerably more work for you and your team.

There are examples of artists who have successfully crowdfunded significant amounts of money, where a part of that success can be attributed to the novelty of the funding method, thus attracting media coverage that, in turn, contributes to the success of the campaign. The novelty would quickly wear off if everybody crowdfunded, potentially causing crowdfunding fatigue among the press and public. Author Miranda Ward[4] says that the music industry dream of being a star and making your fortune has been extended with crowdfunding

> "the democratised, DIY world sells you a dream too, albeit a potentially more humble one, if it's something humble you're looking for."

Artists can and should be positive about building their future career through crowdfunding. As you will see in the case studies in this chapter, crowdfunding success is absolutely achievable, but it is not an easy option – it requires lots of time, effort and creativity, with no guarantee of success. This is the same for offline methods of crowdfunding as well.

WHERE CAN YOU GO TO CROWDFUND?

Crowdfunding platforms are well known to the music industry, and many music companies and musicians have recently completed their first campaign or are considering starting one. The largest and most relevant platforms that artists will want to compare are Kickstarter, Indiegogo and Pledge Music[5]. Alternatives are referenced later on in this chapter.

1. Kickstarter

Launched in April 2009, New York-based Kickstarter became available in the UK in October 2012. In 2013, Kickstarter claimed users had raised over $500 million on the platform. Describing itself as a 'funding platform for creative projects', it is probably the best known of all the crowdfunding sites, and has been used, it says, by around three million 'funders'. Aside from music, some of the other popular categories include documentary films, computer games and technology.

At the time of writing, the site has been used to fund about 7,000 music projects to the tune of $42 million, including performances of new opera, the recording of albums, touring and songwriting.

The best-known music project was run by Amanda Palmer, raising over one million dollars in 2012 to fund her record, art book and tour.

Her background includes working as a street performer/busker, crowdsourcing elements of her work, and couch surfing (staying with fans while touring), all of which she said helped her to ask fans for contributions without feeling bashful. Added to this, Palmer had had a record deal previously, and had spent a long time building up a strong fanbase prior to the campaign both online and through touring. These factors helped her become one of the most successful and high profile crowdfunders to date. To illustrate just how rare her achievement is, in 2012 she was one of 17 of a total of 18,000 projects including non-music ones (less than 0.1 per cent of the total projects) that raised over a million dollars on Kickstarter. She was subsequently able to have mainstream success with a Top 10 album in the USA. Projects like hers have contributed hugely to crowdfunding's credibility in music, and enhanced Kickstarter's reputation.

As the biggest and best-known crowdfunding platform, Kickstarter is a site that many users feel offers consumer awareness and traffic that can help them attract new supporters. However, most of the crowdfunders I have interviewed in relation to reward-based platforms comment that the overwhelming majority of their money came from existing fans, friends, and people in their extended circle of contacts, rather than strangers. Interviewees also indicated that exposure in the mainstream media such as radio play were significant boosters of donations from existing fans.

Kickstarter may reject your project if it does not adhere to its rules. Projects cannot be charitable, either directly or indirectly (including charity records), and must be based in the 'creative arts'. You must also be resident in or have a registered company in one of the countries that Kickstarter has launched. You may want to submit your idea to the site in brief, and well in advance of launch, in case you are not accepted. The projects that feature on its homepage are chosen by staff, but there is also an algorithm that displays popular projects.

It is important to consider carefully the level of funding that you will try to raise, as Kickstarter will only take the money from donors once you reach the target you set at the outset. In the case studies included in this chapter, you will see some examples of targets that particular artists have set, and how they reached them.

The site charges 5 per cent commission on donations to successful projects, and charges 3–5 per cent transaction fees for debit and credit cards, which are processed by Amazon. This increases the mass-appeal potential of the site, as it makes it very easy for the millions of registered Amazon customers to contribute easily.

At the time of writing, Kickstarter has been active for less than a year in the UK, and as such, it is still more established in the US; for example there are over 1,500 projects open for funding in Brooklyn, New York, but fewer than 100 for the whole of London. While some commentators in the US have noted the beginnings of crowdfunding fatigue, Kickstarter has barely penetrated the European market.

There is something appealingly transparent and democratic about the idea of crowdfunding that relies on the creativity and commitment of the artist and support team.

2. Indiegogo

Headquartered in San Francisco, Indiegogo was launched in 2008 by former investment industry worker and theatre buff, Danae Ringlemann. Unlike Kickstarter, it allows charitable fundraising and businesses of all kinds to run campaigns.

Indiegogo emphasises its transparency, providing a lot of helpful information on what makes a campaign successful to help crowdfunding hopefuls develop their campaign. One of its core values is 'equality of opportunity', and the company's founder notes that while female owned businesses only get 3 per cent of venture capital funding from investment firms, women lead about 40 per cent of the companies successfully crowdfunded through Indiegogo.

The so-called 'go-go factor' is Indiegogo's algorithm that determines the placing of your project on the site, influenced by activity around a campaign. Ringelmann says:

> "Success is really based on your hard work and how engaged your audience is."

However, she goes on to say:

> "When a project doesn't raise any money, we don't consider that a failure, it's an incredible learning experience... they may have their marketing message wrong, their product wrong, or not have worked really hard or found an audience that cares about their product – better that they find that out early on..."

While many of the artists I spoke to felt that a crowdfunding campaign felt like begging for money, Ringlemann reframes this:

> "The whole point of the crowdfunding campaign is not to talk about yourself, but to talk about what ideas need to exist in the world, and how others can help it happen. You are the leader or the ambassador of this movement, for your community. The key to success is that people fund the person because they believe in their

vision and what they are trying to accomplish, and believe they can get it done."

She feels that this way of presenting artistic work is actually much closer to the way artists actually work, rather than having to present it directly to investors:

> "In the pitch, you don't need to put on a suit and sell the ROI[6] value of your album… if you have to talk to someone about investing in you, you have to give a different sort of a talk which is a bit less comfortable for artists, in a way, because you have to come up with a profit reason for them to invest."

Indiegogo confirmed that they have in the region of "7,000 campaigns running at any one time" (across all categories) and process "millions of dollars a week."[7]

The Indiegogo Field Guide, available from its website, is a very helpful manual for crowdfunding campaigns on the platform, and its official blog also offers a lot more context and discussion.

3. Pledge Music

UK-based Pledge Music was originally set up by musician Benji Rogers in 2009. The site has now established itself in the USA, with offices in New York, Los Angeles and Boston, and also in Europe and Australia.

Pledge Music was originally set up as a means for independent artists to secure funding from their fans, but it now also works with larger acts who are without a record deal. Pledge Music assesses artists who want to raise money on the site. It will look at metrics such as the artist's engagement with fans on Facebook or the number of active fans on their mailing list to make sure that artists are not asking for a lot more money than they are likely to achieve. Malcolm Dunbar, Pledge Music's MD says that his team use an algorithm which, based on fan engagement across your email, Facebook and Twitter accounts, can calculate a very conservative spend-per-fan conversion rate.

Pledge Music actively helps artists to shape and price their Pledges, based on experience with and closeness to the music industry. Dunbar says:

> "In the last year, between 30 to 40 bands went on to sign with a label or a distributor either during or post [their Pledge] campaign and then dovetailed seamlessly into a conventional release strategy. We've also become chart-eligible in the last year or two, so that music sales that are within a Pledge campaign count towards the UK charts."

Pledge Music charges more than some other sites, with a commission rate of 15 per cent of the total raised, but this includes the credit card charges and hands-on support. Because it specialises in music, it can help artists find partners for manufacturing and fulfilment, for example.

A statement from Pledge said that it has funded over 1,000 artists over a four-year period, and has had in excess of 475,000 pledgers. It is currently running 140 campaigns and completing about four or five each day.

TIPS AND TRICKS ON PLANNING YOUR CROWDFUNDING CAMPAIGN

1. Use self-help guides

There are some excellent guides available from the various crowdfunding platforms. They all describe a series of steps, including:

• developing the basic idea

• knowing your customer and planning your perks/rewards to suit them

• having a creative 'story' and communication plan

• using statistical and qualitative feedback to improve the campaign

• working out how you will deliver pledges on time and on budget.

2. Work on your pitch

Why is your project something you feel passionate about? What difference will it make to you to be able to complete it?

3. How are you going to present the idea?

What language will you use to pitch your 'ask' – will it be witty or serious? Consider making a video. Try some of these ideas out with your support team (manager and label people or friends and supporters).

4. Who are your fans?

What sort of rewards/goods/credits would they like and what can they afford? Will each reward return a profit? Have you got something that allows people with a small budget to participate? Are you able to create a high-ticket item? Will you allow donations?

Offering a range of different tiers of rewards allows you to realise the most income from a campaign.

5. Fulfilment

Work out how you are going to fulfil everything you've committed to deliver. Don't forget to factor in travel and equipment costs for a gig at a funder's house, or fulfilment costs for your merchandise or album. In your budget, do not forget to deduct commission fees, payment processing fees, charity donations and VAT from your gross income.

6. Timeline

How long will take to engage with individual fans and create updates? Will you need any help?

7. Wider considerations

Are you going to build on your crowdfunding campaign by generating broadcast and performance royalties, touring income, online sales or licensing income? If so, when will related activities happen and how will they be carried out? For example, will you be launching a single alongside the campaign to raise money for the album, or going on tour to capitalise on the campaign?

8. Platform and structure

What is the right platform and the right company structure (sole trader, limited company, charity etc.), to be able to meet your goals?

Crowdfunding provides an opportunity for musicians and small music businesses to test the water with a variety of projects before committing money to them. Is there an audience for the music? Can you market well using both social and mainstream media? Can you tell a good story about your project? Can you create the right products and can they be fulfilled? A project might not be a failure even if you fall short in one of these areas, but that area will need to be addressed either by bringing someone with that skillset on-board or learning to do it yourself. Hopefully you will realise this before you have a garage full of stock and no way to distribute it.

OTHER KEY CROWDFUNDING PLATFORMS

My Major Company

A 'fan-funded music' company established in France, in 2007, that has a distribution arrangement with Warner Music France. Users invest money in artists in return for a share of album sales.

Sellaband

A site based in Germany that lets investors buy 'parts' in an artist, which can then be used for a recording project.

Slicethepie

Launched in 2007 as a site that helped unsigned artists raise funding for their recordings, but has since changed its focus to getting fans to listen to and review new music.

Pleasefund.Us

A platform that raises money for creative projects, charities and other good causes.

Peoplefund.It

A site funding start-up businesses, creative projects and social enterprises with advisors including WeFundIt, Crowdcube and Unbound. Hugh Fearnley-Whittingstall is one of the high-profile people involved.

Sponsume

Multi-currency platform (21 to date) for artistic and entrepreneurial projects that lets you access payments immediately.

Buzzbnk (Social Enterprises) Crowdfunding website which enables social entrepreneurs to raise money including donations, loans and profit sharing arrangements.

Spacehive (Local Projects)

A site for funding civic projects in your local area.

Rockethub

A site funding art, science, business and social projects, including a partnership with A&E TV that helps showcase projects.

Wefund

A British site that helps raise money and find audiences for creative projects.

FURTHER READING

Working The Crowd (NESTA, 2013)

A short guide providing an overview of crowdfunding, the different versions of the model and how they work.

Fk The Radio, We've Got Apple Juice, Miranda Ward and Little Fish (Unbound, 2013)**

An account of a DIY artist, comprising a mixture of musings, interviews and stories about being signed versus doing it on your own.

SIX

Sponsorship

This chapter begins with a case study on a brand ambassador deal, Vision Artists and Carl Barât (case study F below) and moves on to look specifically at money from commercial brands that is paid to artists and music companies in return for an association or partnership with the brand. Through the insights and expertise of sponsorship-brokers Ronnie Traynor, Natasha Kizzie and Wendy Smithers, it considers the various features of brand partnerships in music, offers tips for artists and music companies looking for sponsorship, complete with a branding glossary. It ends with a list of research resources available to improve your awareness of brand activity and the key agencies.

CASE STUDY F: VISION ARTISTS AND CARL BARÂT

Matt Luxon of Vision Artists took over the management of Carl Barât, former member of Dirty Pretty Things and The Libertines, around 2009. The management company is part of the same group as a music sponsorship agency, and so is well connected with brands.

Luxon was approached by Philips, the electrical goods company, in the early part of 2011 with a possible endorsement deal for Carl Barât. Philips was launching a new product in its range of Fidelio docking station speakers, and wanted to run a campaign in June of that year to publicise the product.

The theme of the campaign was to be 'Obsessed with Sound': Philips wanted to associate its brand's benefit of high-quality sound with an artist's need for and appreciation of excellent sound quality, thereby building credibility for the product.

Matt Luxon says:

> "They approached me two to three months ahead of launch to see if Carl would be interested. It's a good product category for someone like Carl. He had a look and saw it was a good product, and he was up for endorsing it."

The commercial terms of the agreement were negotiated by Luxon. The key issues for him as a manager were the fee, securing approval on headlines (but not the content) of press articles: and reducing the 'service days' required of the artist. Service days are the number of days the artist has to be available to promote the product by doing interviews, performances, photo calls and press conferences.

Barât had to provide three to four service days as part of the deal, mainly to carry out interviews, and the coverage appeared across a four-month period in Summer 2011. There was no TV advertising connected with the campaign, and although there was a press advertisement, the campaign was mainly driven through 'below the line' activity, including print, online and radio interviews.

There was one restriction on the artist, which was that he had to give exclusivity within the 'home speaker systems/stereo systems' retail category throughout the four months of the campaign, and for a minimum of three months afterwards.

The final service day was a live performance in London (four songs). The brand got three benefits from this:

• Footage and images of the show, which could be distributed online via social media sites and editorial news sites.

• A unique and powerful experience for the national, online, consumer and music journalists who would attend the gig, which would encourage them to write about both Barât's music and the product.

• Media interviews, which took place on the night, in which the benefits of the Fidelio range were discussed and the campaign's message was put across.

Because this deal was a brand ambassador arrangement, the artist needed to communicate the brand's message of being 'Obsessed with Sound' through his press interviews and ideally his personal Twitter feed, during the campaign.

I asked Luxon how this was actually delivered:

> "Carl's not going to say anything he doesn't want to say… and the brand is always trying to get [its] messages across, but we put things into context so Carl could talk about his record and mention the campaign."

Asked in an interview for thisisfakediy.co.uk (June 2011) why the product had his backing, Barât's response was a good example of how to honour brand commitments without compromising integrity.

> "It's a good speaker that they've got there. I listen to it in the bath. It's always a room of joy! Well, it's a good thing and it's about as corporate as I want to get on this, but I think it shows how technology has come so far for something to sound as good and accurate as it is."

Matt planned some of Barât's music activity to coincide with the campaign: "The publisher was very positive and the label, PIAS, were very supportive…"

For example, the label launched a single on the night of the gig and also arranged for a digital EP with extra tracks to be released during the campaign. This strategy helped both the brand and the artist. It created the opportunity to refresh sales of Carl Barât's music and the fact that there was new music coming out from the artist added credibility to the brand because there was something newsworthy happening alongside the launch. Additionally, putting the two together meant that the music press was more likely to cover the brand, and the consumer media and broadsheets that may have already written about the artist used the angle of the product launch and gave him additional exposure. "The brand were very strong on PR, which gave us another stab at press" says Luxon.

This campaign is a great example of a partnership that created a valuable source of non- recoupable money for the artist, and where the product and the artist were appropriately paired.

WHAT IS SPONSORSHIP?

Music sponsorship is a fee paid by a company in return for the commercial benefit of being associated with an artist and the artist's music, or a music brand such as a festival. Sponsorship can be in cash or in kind, meaning given in goods or services. For a long time, a typical music sponsorship was a brand displaying its logo in the background while an artist was performing, and that certainly still exists, but music sponsorship now operates in more sophisticated ways.

It is often described using the broader phrase 'brand partnership' rather than 'sponsorship', to reflect companies' increasing expectation that they will be working collaboratively with the artist, rather than just slapping their logo on something the artist has already created. The sponsor may expect to receive commercial benefits ranging from increased overall brand awareness, improved or shifted association with a particular demographic, to the direct encouragement of sales.

Unlike grants or investment, sponsorship isn't something for which you fill in an application form or complete a business plan. There aren't regimented guidelines and the whole process can seem quite opaque. I therefore decided to seek advice from a number of people with experience of successfully creating deals between sponsors or brands and music.

Natasha Kizzie has 15 years' experience as a brand consultant, including many years at agency KLP (now Arnold KLP). Her role was to work with companies that wanted to launch a brand, create awareness of their new brand, or which had an existing brand that needed repositioning and/or refreshing – for example, if it had gained a negative association among consumers, or had lost relevance as its customers had grown older or as rival brands had entered the market.

Ronnie Traynor works for Vision Artists, an agency that represents artists in deals with brands. A similar role is often fulfilled by a record label, publishing company, live agent or management company negotiating directly with the brand. Vision Artists is a specialist agency which offers a one-stop shop for brands which need to deal with artists, management, labels and publishers. It handles issues such as music rights and co- ordination with touring or promotion activity. The agency has its own database of a few hundred artists with whom it works, including information pertinent to brands seeking the right match.

Wendy Smithers, Director of The Hub, has successfully secured sponsorship for many music events and education programmes that The Hub has developed, both non-profit-making and for-profit. She has also developed fundraising strategies for clients, in order to prepare them to pitch for public funding, private donations and sponsorship.

It was clear from speaking to these experts that there is no one guaranteed formula to securing sponsorship. While there are things that can be done to better position yourself or your music business in relation to sponsors, the main thing that will bring them in is creating a buzz. Once you have an audience that sponsors might want to reach, opportunities will present themselves.

Whatever stage you're at as an artist or music business, it is important to understand what sponsors are looking for from their partnerships.

It works best when your needs are aligned closely with those of the sponsor, yielding mutual benefits as well as valuable income. These three interviewees identified a number of features of successful sponsorship relationships.

1. Be aware of your own brand

Your own brand needs to have achieved some recognition, or you need to be able to convince sponsors of its potential to be a channel for them to reach consumers.

Natasha Kizzie advises that at a minimum, you should be able to demonstrate the strength of your brand and its values through your Twitter following and feed, your Facebook page, YouTube channel, website, blog, email database and newsletter archive. You might not need all of these, or have to have massive numbers, but remember that these channels should and do communicate what you're about and who your audience is to potential sponsors.

'Values' in this context means 'brand values', which could include the overlapping demographics (age, gender, location, purchasing habits) of your fans and of the brand's consumers, and of the issues that concern you that the brand also addresses.

Kizzie explains how a pro-active approach to prove both fan engagement and brand alignment might help when approaching sponsors:

> "Say you're an artist and you've just bought a pair of Adidas trainers, which you love. So you then take a picture of them, tweet it and start thinking about personalising them, and what to do… If you can then measure how many of your fans have engaged with that and say positive things about that brand, you've a piece of homemade research that you can take to that brand and say 'look, 30 per cent of my followers love your brand so much so that they communicated back to me, had something positive to say

about it, and engaged enough that they were actually giving me creative ideas and playing with how they should be interacting with your brand.'"

However, she stressed the need to communicate with an audience in a way that feels personal, natural, organic and appropriate, all the while being aware as to how the information you 'harvest' could be of value to your brand partnership. Kizzie continued:

> "Consider what are your brand characteristics, who is your audience, how are they engaging with you and how are you engaging with them…? They'll want you to have a very clear plan of how you plan to grow your brand, how they can be part of that growth and where they can add value. They will want to work with companies that are reliable, open and transparent."

Vision Artists is an agency that sits between brands (or their agencies) and the music industry. Ronnie Traynor talked about the current market for music/brand partnerships, highlighting their scarcity:

> "Ninety per cent of deals we do are with gold and platinum artists, which you only get when you reach a certain level and brands want to connect with artists."

Its artist database profiles a broad range of artists which it can use when approached by a brand client when planning campaigns. The data includes the demographic of their bands' fans, previous brand partnerships they have held, any restrictions on brands the artists may be willing to work with, or what sorts of deals they may be open to and so-on. For the brands, as well as sourcing the artists, the agency will use its understanding of the music industry to present the brand's offer to artists and ensure that any licensing issues or clashes with the artists' activities are ironed out.

Sponsorship money is probably most appreciated by newer artists, who may tend to be overlooked in favour of artists with a larger audience. One example of opportunities for newer or unsigned artists is some brands' sponsorship of unsigned artists. Traynor says:

> "A few years ago there was an unsigned push but these days, our agency tries to get smaller artists incorporated into brand partnerships alongside more established acts. We always push for lesser-known artists in a show's billing or target a smaller brand. Another example is the mentor programme paid for by Bacardi, where higher profile artists chose up-and-coming acts such as AlunaGeorge and Jessie Ware, and those acts were given a bursary and mentoring. There can be smaller opportunities – managers should keep agencies posted all the time on little bits of support and progress for their artist, as they develop."

You should be able to demonstrate the strength of your brand and it's values through your Twitter following and feed, your Facebook page, YouTube channel, website, blog, email database and newsletter archive.

2. Identifying potential sponsors

The Hub's Wendy Smithers advises that smaller organisations and artists will have to be very focused if they are going to gain sponsorship, and that for smaller amounts of money (between £5,000 and £10,000), applying for grants may well be a better investment of time. However, if a small organisation is going to try to raise sponsorship independently, the most time- consuming part of the process is finding the right people. Smithers says:

> "It's really about using existing networks… to find the right
> person. Even if you think 'oh, I don't know anyone at any
> companies', the chances are if you spread the word out among
> family, friends, colleagues, you are going to get connected."

Social media site LinkedIn and the trade press (Marketing Week, for
example) are great resources for finding out what brands are up to
and finding contacts. The brand manager who has responsibility for
the marketing budget of a product is the best target for a brand
partnership opportunity, but Smithers has found that people in these
positions tend to move around every 6-12 months in large consumer
brand owners such as Diageo and Unilever. In terms of Corporate
and Social Responsibility (CSR)[1] [2]money, she suggests making an
approach to corporate communications managers, or alternatively,
to a company's CEO or Managing Director via their Personal
Assistant.

> "The good thing about a CEO or Managing Director is they tend
> to have a Personal Assistant so however small you are they will
> acknowledge you and they will say, 'yes, you can write to us here,'
> or 'no, it's not really worth you writing,' whereas brand managers
> can ignore you and get away with it."

3. Developing a sponsorship proposal and understanding the language of brands

Alongside using your networks to find the best contacts, you have to
present strong ideas. If you have made contact with a potential
sponsor through friends and family, you can try a personal
approach. Smithers says:

"Often you can just speak to them and say, 'we've got this event coming up,' or, 'we're trying to get funding for this, can I run it by you?' At the very least they will give you some feedback with which to refine further pitches. If you are approaching the brand manager of a large brand you have to be aware that they constantly have to sift through proposals. If your approach is unsolicited, you must do your homework thoroughly and demonstrate this with a highly targeted pitch that shows you have understood the brand's objectives."

A sponsorship proposal gives you a chance to explain what you do, who you are, who your audience is, and what opportunities you can offer that are specifically relevant to that brand.

A sponsorship proposal gives you a chance to explain what you do, who you are, who your audience is, and what opportunities you can offer that are specifically relevant to that brand. You should give details of your audience, the networks with which you are connected, the CSR and PR opportunities for the brand, and any opportunities for employees to get involved with the brand partnership. If the brand belongs to a major company, Smithers recommends that the majority of the proposal should be focused on talking about the brand and how it can deliver what the brand's overseers need. With smaller companies, or ones where you already have an interested contact, there is more scope to talk about your own project.

When pitching for sponsorship, whether in writing or in person, the distinctiveness and commitment that you show will be key to winning support. Smithers says:

"The artist, the festival manager – whoever it is – has got to be eloquent and passionate about what they do, because that's very infectious. The whole pitching element is really key, so to actually get somebody excited about what you do … that will convert into support."

4. Developing commercial terms, delivery and reporting

These days, commercial brands often want to collaborate with music brands or artists on the creative aspects of their partnership. How this interaction might develop will be part of a contractual negotiation between the artist's representative and the brand, based on commercial terms, setting out the nature of the exchange between the two parties. Kizzie says:

> "The brand should be coming to the table with a creative vision of what they want to achieve, based on marrying up the objectives and the values. It helps if you [the musical half of the partnership] come to the table with some ideas – some really innovative ideas that can get both parties excited. Out of that you're going to build some commercial terms, and you then want some time with the artist to actually craft it, and make sure you've really got their commitment and their buy-in, and that they're excited about what you're talking about."

This will be the time for a discussion about what content the brand might want from the deal, and what access they will want to an artist or event and their media channels. If there are any limits to what you are willing or able to do, these should be discussed and negotiated early on. Smithers explains that at the start of the relationship an agreement would be made that detailed, for example, the size and placement of the brand's logo on visual material, the number of free tickets or music to be given away, and what access the brand would have to behind-the-scenes interviews or other such content for the campaign.

Once the deal is signed, there will be a planning stage where timelines are set out and everything is detailed. If the campaign is of short duration, for example if the brand simply wants the artist to appear at an event or give away some content, then this might be relatively routine to execute. On the other hand, a more inventive campaign involves a lot more planning. Kizzie says:

"From there on, I would meet with the rights holder every two weeks and once in the thick of the campaign – every week. That could be with artist management, the label or whoever's been designated as being responsible [for artist-brand liaison]."

During the campaign, everything would be managed and monitored by the brand and its agency in conjunction with the artist. Kizzie says:

"I would be looking at the plan, assessing where we are [in relation to the plan], reviewing what's achieved, what's worked, what's not worked, and how we take the successful stuff and build on that."

Smithers agrees that the deal needs to be clear about how the agreement will be managed in terms of servicing and communication.

"Within that agreement there should be some achievable aims and a clear mechanism to measure effectiveness. In building up trust, communication is absolutely key, because that enables you to better deal with things should they go wrong. If you can do that successfully, then obviously you're more likely to take them with you onto the next project."

There is also a possibility that the campaign might need to be adjusted to react to the interim results or to changes as the campaign plays-out. Kizzie says:

"That's not easy for a lot of brands to do, because they're planning so far ahead having agreed their budget and calculated their return on investment accordingly, but certainly when you get into a relationship with artists, and maybe the creative process and creating music together, it's great just being able to take advantage of the special things that [spontaneously] happen: to say 'we're in a partnership, we should be able to do this with you' – it benefits your brand, and vice versa."

At the end of the campaign, evaluation by the brand manager would be typically expected to demonstrate the impact of the brand's spending against the objectives of the campaign. Media equivalency values may be used to quantify the value of the campaign in terms of what the results would have cost the brand in terms of advertising spend. For example, press and online coverage of the activity, social media activity, posts and comments on YouTube etc. will reach a certain number of people (known as 'eyeballs'). The equivalent exposure achieved through conventional advertising spend might in theory have cost the brand considerably more. There are other benefits of using brand activity in conjunction with music artists. For example, rather than just seeing a piece of advertising, by experiencing and participating in campaign activity, it is felt that the consumer has had a deeper and more meaningful encounter with the brand. The campaign may have improved the awareness or perception of the brand which can be measured through market research.

And hopefully, other than financially, the artist or music business will have benefitted from the campaign, too.

A BRANDING GLOSSARY (FOR THE UNINITIATED)

Whilst Natasha Kizzie recommends being authentic as an artist or organisation – which suggests not being concerned with artificially becoming a 'marketing platform' – you will find that a lot of branding language gets used once you start a dialogue with brands or their agencies.

Here are some of the phrases that you will hear or see in discussions with brands and their agencies.

Activation

Activation is the part of a campaign where, after all the planning, the customer or fan gets to interact with the brand through some sort of online or offline participation.

Amplification

Getting engaged users to spread your message (or the brand's message). The brand would ideally want your fans to talk about the campaign on social media and via word-of-mouth, which will increase the attention that it gets beyond what can be achieved by advertising.

Brand ambassador

An artist or other individual who will speak for the brand in public and support its product, service or values. Often used by charities (e.g. United Nations Goodwill Ambassadors) but also by a brand when it is basing its campaign around an individual, and wants what the individual says to be consistent with the brand's message.

Brand values

What the brand stands for. This is sometimes supplemented by a 'brand personality', which is normally described using adjectives. For example a brand such as Apple might describe itself as Irreverent, Reliable, Friendly, Modern and Simple. This personality will be communicated by the product itself and all the marketing surrounding it, including the shops, staff, and of course sponsorship partners. Brands also profile in detail the demographic of the typical or target users. For example, it may look at where these users socialise, what they read, the music they listen to, the other consumer products they use and so on.

Brand messaging

Communication of the brand's values, which can come across in both obvious ways (such as broadcasting an advert or displaying a slogan) or subtly, through the way a campaign is implemented.

Channel

The means by which a message is communicated by the artist or brand. This could include television adverts, social media, etc.

Content

Could be music content, such as an exclusive piece of music given away by the brand, or other digital material that can be distributed to fans.

Experiential marketing

This is brand/artist activity that goes beyond advertising and involves consumers or fans in some sort of activity that makes them feel positively about the brand. This could include an event, competition, interaction with the artist or brand online, a live gig, a flashmob – the ways of creating this interaction are endless.

FMCG (Fast Moving Consumer Goods)

High-volume, mass market products such as soft drinks, washing powder, food brands, toiletries, etc. that are competed over fiercely by different brands, and therefore rely on high marketing spends to achieve sales.

Leveraging the artist/fan relationship

Using the already existing relationship between artists and their fans to achieve an objective such as getting people talking about the brand.

Multi-channel assets

Likely to be pieces of media which can be used across a number of channels (see above) such as photographs, video of a performance, an interview with the artist, digital parts of a track to be given away and remixed or a text interview with an artist. The assets can be used to deliver a campaign that will get fans involved.

Platform

A dedicated place for the brand/artist relationship to be communicated, such as a standalone website, event or other access point.

Sponsorship property

An event, tour, experience, project, piece of media, relationship or image that sponsorship can be sold against.

TIPS ON WORKING WITH BRANDS

1. Understand your own brand

What are you about? What marketing channels have you built up? How do you see your own brand growing?

2. Build relationships with brands

Court them. Share your music and your enthusiasm and make them part of your journey, keeping them updated without becoming a nuisance.

3. Be yourself and be original

Don't be generic, or try to be exactly the same as the brand you want to attract.

Smithers suggests that despite a recent trend for brands to create their own events, the distinctiveness and authenticity of events created by the music industry keeps them coming back for quality branding opportunities.

4. Know your limits

Without coming across as difficult, "know how much you're willing to give away, and what you're not willing to give away," says Kizzie. Don't be subservient; willingly fulfil the contract, but don't get pushed into over-delivering.

Ronnie Traynor advises artists to be clear about what the requirements are, only work with brands that they want to work with, and to only sign up to a project if they feel completely happy about it.

· · ·

5. Use what the brand can bring to the table

This may include communications or design expertise. Be clear in your mind how that's enabling you to move your brand forward.

6. Be open to collaboration with the brand

Find out whether there is potential to create something interesting with them, before starting to negotiate terms, advises Kizzie.

7. Examine your brand partners

Kizzie's advice is to do your homework. Look at their media profile, how frequently they are communicating with their audience and what people are saying about them. Visit their website, read their annual report, learn what they have achieved that year and learn about any forthcoming strategic objectives. All of this can help you understand their needs in the partnership, and where you can add value.

8. Network

Go to conferences and events that brand managers attend to find out about music: Amsterdam Dance Event, International Music Summit in Ibiza, MIDEM or SXSW. All are great places to meet potential sponsors, as are specific brand agency events and conferences.

9. Do background reading to understand the marketing world

Kizzie recommends observing positively talked-about campaigns, and whether elements of these could be built into a proposal.

10. Have a clear structure in place

Work out how and when you will be reporting back to the brand,

and how their requests will be responded to. It's important if you are much smaller than your brand partner that you have the resources to do this.

MUSIC SPONSORSHIP RESOURCES

Campaign

Trade publication for advertising and branding. Contains links to many featured adverts and online campaigns.

Contagious

Online resource for brands, following strategies, technologies and trends.

Creative Review

Covers trends in advertising, design and visual culture.

Marketing

Magazine site for marketing professionals that will help you identify brand managers and the latest brand news.

Music Activation

Collects and collates noteworthy activations by brands in the field of music.

Universal Music And Brands

Find out how Universal Music, the biggest record label in the world presents itself to brands on its own website for brand partnerships.

Some Brand Agencies: Arnold KLP, Foam London Frukt, Ignite, Vision Artists.

SEVEN

Debt Finance

This chapter explains what debt finance is in a business context, specifically looking at loans and the conditions likely to be applied by lenders. It describes some of the sources of lending that are available to businesses and looks at the process of applying for a loan.

WHAT IS DEBT FINANCE?

Debt finance means using borrowed (loaned) money to finance a business activity, for which interest is paid to the lender in addition to the loaned sum being repaid. This form of funding could be deployed at many different stages in a company's development, for example at the start-up stage of the business to help cover the initial costs, to provide working capital in order to expand, or to cover the cash flow requirements of the business.

I have found two typical responses to debt among small music business owners. The first is to be very wary and cautious, because of fears that it may cripple the business. This concern is compounded by the fact that taking out a business loan, as well as giving the business another fixed cost to pay, also typically means using your home (if you own it) or other personal assets to guarantee the loan. Many home-owning directors would prefer to borrow the money from their mortgage company, giving it as a director's loan to their company, than pay the arrangement fees and interest rates of a bank loan and become indebted to their bank.

The second response is an enthusiasm for debt as being preferable to equity. Fiercely independent business owners tend not to want to have to take on investors who might wish to become involved with the running of the business. They might also not want to grow the company as aggressively as an investor might require. For them, the anonymity of a bank is preferable to the presence of an investor.

In this chapter I focus on loans – money borrowed for a fixed time period within an agreed repayment schedule, but I want to briefly mention some of the other types of business debt:

1. Mortgages

These are very commonly used to deal with a long-term purchase of assets such as business premises.

2. Overdrafts

These are a short-term measure for flexible bank borrowing for managing the ups and downs of cash flow.

3. Credit Cards

These, again, are a short-term form of finance that can help manage cash flow and small purchases more efficiently than cash.

. . .

4. Trade Credit

This the period your suppliers might give you to pay money owed, which again helps with cash flow.

All of these are forms of credit that an incorporated business can take out in its own name. However it is not uncommon for business owners to be asked to guarantee a business debt or to borrow money in their personal name, and invest that money in developing their business. They might choose to borrow against the equity in their home, or use a personal loan to put money into their company because they are able to access lower interest rates, easier terms or simply because they cannot secure a loan in the name of the business.

If you take out loan as a sole trader, you are personally liable for this because, as detailed in the Business Organisation chapter, your business is considered the same 'legal entity' as you.

SMALL MUSIC BUSINESSES AND BANK LOANS

It is extremely tough for either small music businesses without a strong trading history or for individual musicians to access business loans. Arguably this has always been the case for any small business, and certainly in recent years, with the tightening of credit for all businesses, the situation has clearly worsened.

The high street retail banks – by far the largest lenders – come under the greatest scrutiny of their lending procedures, and have lately been heavily criticised by business organisations and the Government for not doing enough to lend to small businesses.

The Federation of Small Businesses' Voice of Small Business Index for Quarter 1 (2013) asked a regularly surveyed panel of members if they had applied for credit in that quarter, 19.8 per cent of those surveyed had, and of these 41 per cent were successful, 41.8 per cent were unsuccessful and 17 per cent were awaiting a decision.

Contrastingly, the British Bankers' Association's data reveals approval rates of 73 per cent for loans and 74 per cent for overdrafts as applied for by smaller businesses in Q1 of 2013.

The Federation of Small Businesses' 2012 UK Membership survey states:

> "There is little evidence in the figures to suggest that Project Merlin[1], the agreement between the Government and four of the major high street banks to promote lending to small businesses, has been successful in widening the availability of finance.
>
> Seventy per cent of members claim to have used finance to support their main business over the past 12 months, 19 per cent fewer than in 2009."

In 2010 the Music Managers Forum (MMF) took the lead on this issue. Their Chairman Brian Message of ATC group tested claims that the Government's Enterprise Guarantee Scheme (EFG) was open to 'own-account musicians' by operating a test case with The Rifles – a band with whom he was working. The band applied to the four major high street banks for a £200,000 loan to finance an album and tour, and were declined in each case. Reasons given included that they did not have enough trading history, were too risky because they had included overseas trade in their plan, or that music as a sector was just too risky.

Another example illustrating the hurdles small businesses can face in accessing loans on the high street is that of Sam McGregor's Signature Brew, a company that produces craft beers created by different bands (see featured case study in the next chapter on Investment). Sam and his fellow directors approached five different retail banks over a four- month period, and made two full applications.

The directors were well received by the majority of bank staff with whom they met, who seemed to really understand their product, their business and their plan. McGregor says:

> "Most of the people we met were really [understanding] – you go in there, you don't know who you're going to meet. One of the things we asked them was 'do you like beer?' One of them was really into it, had loaned to a few craft beer businesses and seemed to know the market really well. One lady we dealt with emailed me the next day saying she'd taken the beers home to her boyfriend – he loved them – and it helped that they'd all heard of one of the bands."

The directors were able to demonstrate a growing market for their product, and presented very detailed plans for how they were going to use the money to fund the development, manufacturing and marketing of their stock. The bank staff also helped them to improve their cash flow forecasts and gave them feedback that the business owners were able to use to refine and strengthen their applications. Unfortunately, they were not successful in either application. McGregor says:

> "The hardest thing for me was that we were so well received; I went in and presented the documents and I thought, 'I've got to be better than most of the people that come in here, because I've done all this properly' only to then be turned down. I was

surprised, because they were so positive to begin with. It wasted a lot of our time and it was just frustrating."

The specific feedback on why they had been rejected was, according to McGregor, quite vague. He mentioned three specific points: (i) that they were categorised as being in the retail sector, which was felt to be high risk; (ii) that they were lacking security for the loan (all three directors were quite young, and did not own property); and (iii) that there was not enough background on the directors (again, age conspired against them and none of them had worked in either the brewing or retail business before). So while it is clear that obtaining a loan for a small music business will be a challenge, this chapter looks at some of the options available.

WHERE CAN YOU GET LOANS?

The three main sources of loans are high street banks (often referred to as retail banks), community finance organisations and peer-to-peer lending. Borrowing from individuals, which is also a valid source of loans, is explored in the earlier chapter on Friends and Family.

1. High Street Banks

There are four big banking groups in Britain: Lloyds Banking Group, Royal Bank of Scotland Group (including NatWest and Coutts), HSBC and Barclays. Other important bank lenders include Santander, Standard Chartered, The Co-operative Bank, Metro bank, Yorkshire Bank and Aldermore. Each of these banks offer banking facilities to small businesses, including loans, overdrafts, credit cards and sometimes invoice financing or 'factoring' (when cash is exchanged upfront against the value of invoices issued to customers), and also hire-purchase or fixed asset loans to buy equipment or machinery.

While there are certainly some music industry businesses that depend on fixed assets (recording studios, large-scale touring and manufacturing), the music sector deals mainly in either services (live performances) or intangible assets (music copyright, goodwill in a festival brand) which can be difficult to value. Additionally, for many businesses (record labels and music publishers, management companies and artists) it is difficult to forecast sales and cash flow accurately, and a long time can elapse between releasing recordings or publishing music and deriving an income.

Therefore the industry's greatest need is for money to meet short-term working capital requirements, and to finance the development and marketing of products and services. It has never been easy for the industry to obtain bank loans, partly because the music business is poorly understood by banks[2], partly because it can be speculative and risky[3] and partly because of the lack of fixed assets and reliable cash flows.

High street lenders are extremely cautious about lending to small businesses in general, and with the music industry in a challenging state anyway, the chances of a small music business getting a loan from a high street bank are very low. If you are going to approach them, bear in mind that you are more likely to get a loan with the bank you already hold your business account with. Nevertheless, do shop around. The British Bankers Association offers a loan-finder search facility, and some of the comparison sites also offer this service. You can also ask locally about active and supportive business banking managers or ask your bank if they have a centralised media banking unit (possibly only suitable if you are an established business).You may want to consider transferring your account to another branch or a different bank to get the right loan.

Going into the bank you will need to be well prepared and you should expect to have to present a convincing and clear explanation of why you want the loan and how you will use it, demonstrate that you have good financial systems, good management, a good business plan, a strong set of accounts and a cash flow forecast. However, your sector may still push the level of risk beyond what the bank is willing to accept. It is possible to obtain unsecured loans, in which case you will probably be asked for a personal guarantee. If your own credit record and ability to repay were not evidenced, then you would be highly unlikely to get an unsecured loan. In those circumstances you would almost certainly then be asked to provide security for the loan.

If you do not have assets such as a home or other capital, but the bank is positive about your proposition, then you would, in theory, be eligible to use the Enterprise Finance Guarantee Scheme (EFG) – a government initiative guaranteeing up to 75 per cent of a loan to a viable business without security. Small businesses have always complained about a lack of access to finance and a funding gap. However, following 2008 and the global 'credit crunch,' high street banks were implored by the Government to improve their provision of debt finance to small firms, but also (and contradictorily) to recapitalise and build up their reserves of cash, i.e. hold on to more money.

The EFG is part of the Government's contribution to helping the flow of credit to small businesses. The Department of Business Innovation and Skills says:

> "The Enterprise Finance Guarantee programme helps business without sufficient track record or collateral to access loans and currently supports £1.7 billion of SME lending that would otherwise not have been made."[4]

However the EFG does not necessarily make the banks any less cautious about lending to small businesses. Although up to 75 per cent of an individual loan may be secured by this scheme, less than 10 per cent of a bank's total EFG-secured debts can be reclaimed from government. So the risk to them is only slightly lessened, and they are still exposed to over 90 per cent of the value of these loans. However, if you feel that you are only slightly under the threshold for securing a loan, you could ask to apply for a loan under the EFG scheme. If you apply for a loan to one of the high street banks, and are not accepted, be aware that you can now appeal against its decision.

If you are offered a loan (or other credit) you should read the small print and get an idea of what the terms and conditions might be before proceeding with the application. For example, what are the arrangement fees, what is the total cost of the loan including all the interest across its term, can you make overpayments or take repayment holidays, and are there any fees for late or early repayment of the loan? An advantage of a loan is that provided you don't default on the repayments, it is not repayable on demand (unlike an overdraft) and so the credit will be available to you over an agreed period of years to manage the repayments. Additionally, the interest rates will almost certainly be lower than a credit card.

2. Community Finance Organisations

An alternative to loans from retail banks are loans from what are described as 'stakeholder banks' such as co-operatives, credit unions, community development finance institutions (CDFIs) and public savings banks.

The CDFIs are particularly relevant for small businesses. Many CDFIs specialise in offering loans to people who have been declined by the high street banks. CDFIs are not run for profit, and have several advantages over high street banks. They usually offer support and advice alongside their loans, so clients can get help with business planning and sometimes mentoring, before applying for a loan. These loans are normally affordable (although interest-bearing) and offer reasonable and flexible terms and conditions, and they can sometimes offer credit to businesses without security and to people with a poor credit history. For example, some CDFIs specialise in offering loans to people from disadvantaged backgrounds to help them start a business. Furthermore, they can often offer loans to set up social enterprises and not just commercial businesses. An example of this is the East London Small Business Centre, whose website states:

> "We offer a broad range of loan funding to support new start-ups and existing businesses to survive and grow. Our portfolio of loans includes a loan fund for the creative sector, a Sharia-compliant loan and intervention loan funding against order."
>
> ...
>
> "All loan fund clients receive one-to-one business support to help develop and refine clients' business plans, ensuring viability and enhancing the opportunities of access to finance."

The East London Small Business Centre is one of two places that are currently piloting an Arts Council England-backed scheme called Creative Industry Finance, which has offered loans to eight music businesses in its first year (2012–13). This is covered in more detail in the chapter on Grants, but the results so far are promising, and there are hopes that the scheme may be rolled out nationally after the end of the pilot in 2014.

As with a bank loan, business plans, accounts, cash flow forecasts and other checks will be undertaken by a CDFI lender. All the usual caveats apply such as properly checking out all the terms and conditions before taking out a loan, and CDFIs are not as strictly regulated or standardised as banks, so take care to check everything carefully.

Recent statistics show that they are a realistic source of finance for micro-businesses in particular. In 2012, 72 per cent of loan applications to CDFI's were approved, accounting for a total of 2,746 business loans, of which 90 per cent came from micro-businesses[5].

Their trade body, the Community Development Finance Association, states that the average loan to micro-enterprises in 2012 was £10,700, ranging between £1,000 and £30,000 per loan. For SMEs during the same period, the average loan was £45,000, ranging between £25,000 and £103,000 per loan. The average interest rate for micro and SME loans was 12 per cent, again with a range of rates varying from 0–30 per cent. The CDFA offers a website called *Finding Finance* that helps you find a CDFI in your area that offers business loans.

For those aged under 30 in England and Northern Ireland, the government-backed Start Up Loans scheme, which launched in 2012, may offer the opportunity to obtain access to loans. The

Government is making £117.5m available to fund Start Up Loans up to 2015. This scheme may soon be extended to older people, and is offered via a number of providers. It offers personal loans and the average is £5,400 with a fixed rate of six per cent (correct at the time of publication). Unemployed young people who are claimants of Job Seekers Allowance are advised by Start Up Loans to look at a scheme called the New Enterprise Allowance to access a loan to start a business while their unemployment benefits are reduced gradually[6].

These schemes will be joined by the Government's Business Bank, being set up by the Department of Business Innovation and Skills, which says:

> "Business Bank will be a body that manages a suite of established and new business funding and support schemes. We will also commit all £300m of the investment programme by the end of the 2013/14 financial year. It will be set up in 2014."

So the oversight of many of the existing government-backed schemes, supplemented by new schemes, will be consolidated and – it is hoped – should make them easier to access.

3. Peer-To-Peer Lending

More recent entrants into the lending market are crowdfunding-styled peer-to-peer lenders, which have flourished in the last four or five years as banks have retreated from lending and interest rates for savers have been at an historic low. Peer-to-peer lenders are online platforms that arrange for individuals or businesses to lend to one another. The lenders get a higher rate of interest than they would on their savings, and this is normally at a lower overall cost for the borrower than they might get from a bank.

The three largest peer-to-peer lenders are Zopa.com, FundingCircle.com and Ratesetter.com. Together, they have launched the Peer-to-Peer Finance Association to try to establish industry standards as the market expands with new entrants. Its' website states:

> 'The Association has established a wide definition of peer-to-peer finance providers as: "Platforms that facilitate funding via direct, one-to-one contracts between a single recipient and multiple providers of funds, where the majority of providers and borrowers are consumers or small businesses'. Generally, funding is in the form of a simple loan, but other instruments may evolve over time."

To give some idea of the scale of the business, the Open Data Institute has published a report called Show Me The Money, which analyses the data of these three sites, and calculates that between October 2010 and May 2013 these three sites have lent £378 million to 59,581 recipients (both businesses and individuals).

Currently, FundingCircle.com is operating business loans, and Zopa indicated this year that it plans to begin doing so. There are also a number of other providers such as thincats.com that specialise in larger loans or rebuildingsociety.com at the smaller end of the market.

If you wanted to borrow from FundingCircle. com, you would make an online application, which would be reviewed by its underwriters within two working days, to tell you whether or not you can borrow using its platform. If the application is approved, they will allocate you a 'risk band' using your credit score information on Experian[7], ranging from A+ to C−. The website will then create an online loan page for you and run an 'auction' period of 7–14 days where investors can bid on your application (offer you money). Once your loan request is fully funded with bids you can then choose to accept the loan and draw down the money.

FundingCircle.com claims that:

> "Any established and creditworthy business currently operating in the UK can apply for a loan at Funding Circle, including partnerships or limited businesses (unfortunately this excludes sole traders). Businesses must have at least two years of filed accounts or, in the case of companies that do not file accounts, been trading for at least two years, and have no outstanding County Court Judgements over £250."

Business borrowers pay interest to investors and fees to Funding Circle. The company says that interest rates are determined by the risk band you are in, how fully you fill in your loan request page, and how promptly you answer investor questions.

These sites provide a healthy alternative to the big banks, and are being encouraged by the Government which has given them money to lend to SMEs. These peer-to-peer lenders are beginning to disrupt the overall lending landscape, which is an exciting prospect given the complaints from business organisations about a lack of lending by the major banks. However, they are very much commercial operations, and can be selective about their terms. Ratesetter does a credit check, and only accepts about 12 per cent of applications, whilst Thincats.com will only lend to established firms.

They are not willing to take on the risks that either an equity investor or a stakeholder/community bank would. Furthermore, as

they are relatively new, at the time of writing it has not been possible
to establish how suited they may be to the music business sector.

HOW DO LENDERS DECIDE WHETHER TO APPROVE A BUSINESS LOAN?

The five Cs of credit is a commonly used tool to explain what
criteria lenders are looking at when they assess a loan. These are
character, capacity, capital, collateral and conditions.

1. Character

Will you be a reliable person and pay back the loan? The lender has
to make a judgement of this – they might look at your account
history with them and personal credit history. They will want to
know if you have ever been declared bankrupt for example, and
they might look at references from others, or take account of your
industry reputation.

2. Capacity

The ability of the borrower to pay back the loan: what is his/her
cash flow likely to be and what kind of revenues will s/he be able to
generate?

3. Capital

How much is the borrower putting into his/her business from
his/her own money? The lender won't want to be the only one
risking cash.

4. Collateral

Have you or has your business any assets that can be offered to the
lender as security against you defaulting on the loan? For example,

high-value equipment or your house. Alternatively have you a guarantor who will pay the balance owed if you default?

5. Conditions

There are two concerns here – what is the overall financial climate surrounding the lender and your business, and what specifically are you using the loan for? If you are in a growing sector, and your business needs new equipment to expand its activities, you should spell that out. It means the risk is lower to the lender.

In order to assess the five Cs, lenders will want to see evidence such as business accounts, cash flow forecasts, any contracts for work that you may have 'in the pipeline', a business plan, your business banking history, proof of your identify, address and immigration status, details of any personal or business assets that you can use to secure the loan, and a personal credit check.

You will probably have to have a personal meeting with the person approving the loan before your loan is passed to a credit team or assessor to finalise the decision. The cash flow forecast is one of the most important documents in applying for credit, because it is the evidence of how your plans will enable you to make the loan repayments.

If all the evidence adds up to a level of risk that the lender finds tolerable – and they all have different levels of risk they are willing to accept - it may then be possible to access credit. A truism in business is that it is always easy to get loans when you do not need them. The music businesses I have spoken to that own their own premises have a big catalogue of copyrights that generate a steady cash flow, or are awash with investor money, say they would find it easy to access loans - but that they do not need them.

Martin Goldschmidt of independent record label Cooking Vinyl has been in business for more than 25 years. He says:

> "It's very hard when you're starting out. We find it very easy to obtain money from banks, but when I started out it was a complete nightmare. I could only get money when I'd been running a successful business for many, many years."

It can be easier to obtain personal credit than credit for a new business. An incorporated business has its own legal entity, which makes it separate from the people who own or manage it. That means, in principle, that the business can borrow money in its own right. However, a new business has very little financial track record. So compared to an individual whose credit history can be searched and who cannot close down or disappear, there is a much greater risk in business loans for new businesses than for individuals.

TYPICAL CONDITIONS TO LOOK OUT FOR IN A LOAN AGREEMENT

Arrangement Fees

At the Co-operative Bank this is one per cent of the value of the loan, though different elsewhere.

Credit Checks

These will look at business account history and the personal credit position of the directors.

Interest Rates

The risk profile of the loan will impact on the rate.

. . .

Repayment Period

For fixed rate loans of up to £25,000, a term of one to five years to repay the loan is typical. Meanwhile overdrafts can be repayable on demand, but are more flexible on a day-to-day basis to manage short-term cash flow fluctuations. Some lenders will offer variable interest rates and longer repayment periods (often on larger loans).

Principal

The amount the borrower originally takes out, which for most small business loans will be between £2,000 and £25,000.

Secured

If the capital position of the company is weak, personal guarantees from directors or shareholders, or securing the loan against their homes is a typical way of managing lenders' risks.

Payment Holidays

Some loans offer flexibility in when the repayments are made, either in a period at the beginning of the loan term when they do not require any repayments, or at selected periods throughout the term.

PLACES TO LOOK FOR A LOAN

High Street Banks

The British Bankers Association – the trade body for the retail banking sector – contains names and links to its 200 member banks that operate in the UK, including all the big high street names that offer business banking, loans and overdrafts, among them many of the 46 delivery partners of the Enterprise Finance Guarantee Scheme.

Better Business Finance

Better Business Finance is the 'delivery channel' for business finance initiatives arising from the Business Finance Taskforce, and includes tips and information about where and how to look for business finance including government-backed schemes.

ZOPA

Peer-to-peer lender which, at the time of writing, makes only personal loans (which could be put into a business by the borrower) and which recently announced plans to offer business loans, starting with loans to sole traders.

Funding Circle

The Government's Business Finance Partnership scheme (BFP) is lending £20m through Funding Circle. It already offers business loans, and says: "British people have helped to lend nearly £90million to more than 1,700 businesses."

Ratesetter

Entered the peer-to-peer market in October 2010. Rates offered start from 4.8 per cent and borrowers must be at least 24 years old, have a good credit history and a regular income. No business loans – yet.

A Community Finance Organisation

A site that helps users identify loans available from one of the 53 members of the Community Finance Development Association, depending on your regional location. Includes Shariah-compliant products.

. . .

The Prince's Trust Enterprise Programme

Supports unemployed young people aged 18–30 to establish whether their business ideas are viable and if self-employment is right for them.

Start Up Loans Company

A government-funded scheme to provide loans and mentors for new, young entrepreneurs.

It is expected that the scheme will be extended to the over 30s.

Moneyfacts

Comparison website that allows comparisons between business banking products.

Credit Unions

Credit unions are mutual savings and loans institutions, owned by their members. There are almost 500 of these small institutions in the UK with around one million members, and they are set to expand. Legislation introduced in February 2012 enables them to offer products in a way that is more directly comparable to high street lending, and to open up their services to small businesses and community groups as well as to individuals.

EIGHT

Investment

This chapter contains two case studies – Signature Brew (case study G) and Red Grape Records/Jake Morley (case study H) illustrating how seed investment works on a fairly small scale within a micro-business. It considers some of the principles and language of investment, before looking in detail at three different types of investor – venture capital, business angels and investors from your own network – with insights from key investment companies including Ingenious Media and Edge Investments. It concludes with a list of relevant investment companies.

———

CASE STUDY G: SIGNATURE BREW

Sam McGregor had been in bands since the age of 15, playing at small venues all over Europe.

However, it was one small venue in Hull that gave him his business idea. Most venues gave the band a small 'rider' of a crate of beer, usually from one of the big "bland" brands, but the Adelphi venue offered them a box of assorted real ales and a box of curry, a gesture that had remained with him over the years:

> "I went on and did more tours, and never really forgot about that amazing rider. I was tour managing, and saw bands getting better food and staying in good hotels … with racks and racks of champagne, but they were still getting shit beer."

Working with business partner David Riley on social media and direct-to-fan projects, McGregor was always coming up with business ideas and pitching them to Riley:

> "I just put the two together and said 'bands can interact with their fans, why not remedy this problem of not very good beer being given to bands and not very good beer available at gigs and use the direct-to-fan route to market?'"

After bringing onboard his cousin with a background in the brewing industry, the idea began to take shape. Bands signing up with Signature Brew would choose their own beer recipe from a selection presented by a brewery and develop a bespoke beer brand unique to them. It could then be sold wholesale to venues, at artists' shows and direct to the fans via mail order.

THE FIRST BREW

So how did Sam McGregor and his colleagues start to develop the business, based on that original idea? "Before approaching any bands we needed to get a brewery onboard." Their first business plan was quite basic, simply explaining how they would market and sell the idea – luckily it was well received. The first bit of support that McGregor got was credit from suppliers:

> "The brewery was very supportive of what we were doing, they gave us good credit terms and we were able to extend those to a bottling company and a labelling company, so we didn't have to stump up loads of money to begin with. When it did come time to pay them, we still had loads of stock left, so I used my savings of a few thousand pounds."

LOOKING FOR LOANS

The products quickly caught on, and for the first year the business ran alongside the partners' other businesses without additional support. However, in summer 2012 Signature Brew released its third beer, Remedy, with rapper Professor Green. Things were going very well, and it was becoming a lot of work. Sam started to realise that he needed to focus full-time on growing the business before any rivals entered the market, and for that, he would need some funding:

> "We put word around that we were looking for an investor, at the same time as we were applying for loans … so we wrote this big business plan, and then started approaching banks."

McGregor found it hard to estimate how the unit cost would decrease as they increased production, so writing a cash flow forecast covering a three-year period involved making some educated guesses. They also made sure they demonstrated the experience the founders had that was relevant to the running of the business.

As well as the spreadsheets, they included information about the different directors and staff, and the growing market for craft beers. The business made a number of applications for loans at different banks – all of which were declined.

FINDING THE INVESTOR

When it came to finding an alternative investor, things went rather better. Another small business recommended approaching its investor, who was interested in Signature Brew's proposal.

> "Both sides went through a process of scoping each other out. He wanted to see our bank statements and costs: by this time we had a really comprehensive business plan. We asked about his history and how he envisaged working with us, meanwhile we did our due diligence including a Companies House search. He had been an accountant for a merchandising company, something very similar to what we do."

I wondered what attracted the investor. "I guess our work ethic," thinks McGregor, "and although we're quite strong-minded about what we want to achieve, we're … open to new ideas and suggestions."

Signature Brew's original three directors then had to try to value the fledgling business and decide how much they were willing to sell.

> "None of us wanted to own less of the business than the incoming investor, so we set an upper limit of what we were prepared to give away … we agreed an amount of investment [in return] for a percentage of the company, and then [a separate amount as] a

loan with flexible repayment terms ... which protected the investor a little."

The four directors are open and communicative, with the investor having full access to information on the finances, advising on accountancy and tax matters and also helping the company to negotiate some of their deals. Although some businesses prefer to have a 'silent' investor, in this particular case, the investor is very involved in all the business decisions. Despite this the three original directors have structured the deal so that although they need to inform the investor of business decisions, with their collective majority share of ownership they may still act without his agreement.

Signature Brew now has six beer brands on the market, each with a different artist. These include Enter Shikari, whose fans could buy the beer on the band's December 2012 tour. Additionally, Q Magazine created their own beer, Q Red Label, for their awards in October 2012. As well as selling the beer online, over a dozen independent bars stock Signature Brew beers.

SAM MCGREGOR'S TIPS ON LOOKING FOR INVESTORS

1. Provide evidence

Provide factual evidence for everything you claim in your plan, e.g. potential markets for the product.

2. Diversify income streams

Think about what else you could sell around your main product to help build revenues.

3. Find investors close to home

Use your own networks to help find an investor. Get the word out that you are looking for investment.

4. Do due diligence on your investor

Check them out at Companies House and ask for references.

5. Consider what's in it for them

Think about what percentage of your business you are prepared to sell, and how the investor will make their return.

6. Think about your exit strategy

Will you buy your investor out, sell the company, or float it on the stock exchange?

———

CASE STUDY H: REDGRAPE RECORDS AND MANAGEMENT AND JAKE MORLEY

Kerry Harvey-Piper, director of Red Grape Records & Management, was not unfamiliar with the ups and downs of working with city investors. In 2005 she was one of a team developing a musicians' networking site with a small record label as part of the business. But when MySpace suddenly took off at a time when their site was not yet fully developed, the investors got cold feet and pulled out of the deal. Talking about that time, Kerry says:

> "We were left with a situation where we'd got two artists signed to the label, we'd made a lot of good contacts and I'd started to learn how to run a label. I just didn't want to let that experience go."

Although Harvey-Piper had no prior music industry experience, she had worked in marketing, sales and PR, including independent book publishing, which she knew had the same 'do-it-yourself' ethos as the independent music business.

Having set about 'learning the ropes' of running a label, and after a couple of years, she started working as an artist manager. Harvey-Piper explains:

> "One of the artists we'd signed to the label was Hafdis Huld, from Iceland. Her manager decided to leave the business, so I suggested to Hafdis that in the interim, until we found her a new manager, I would take over the day-to-day managerial responsibilities. It worked so well that she never bothered finding another manager."

Since then Harvey-Piper has grown the management side of the business to 80 per cent of what she does, directly managing four artists and advising on the management of two others.

CHANCE MEETING WITH AN INVESTOR

At a gig, one of her clients, Jake Morley, impressed a distributor in the audience who had worked with the Icebreaker investment fund (operated by Shamrock Ltd) on other projects. He bought a copy of the artist's first album, and suggested to Icebreaker that they should consider investing in Morley.

"When someone approaches you, you want to find out who they are," she explains. In addition to checking references, she asked direct questions at meetings that she felt were important: how the funder operated, where their money comes from, the level of returns they expected, what they were looking for out of the deal and how they expected to make their exit at the end of the project.

Describing what investors look for, she observes:

> "They not only have to love what the artist does, they also have to
> feel that the artist has a future, and that the team around the artist
> – the basic manager-label unit – is a team that they want to
> invest in."

PUTTING TOGETHER THE PLAN

Along with the artist's label, Harvey-Piper drew up a budget for a
project she devised with Jake Morley. She was initially unsure as to
the level of funding available, but worked out how much they would
need "to do a great job" at the level that was right for the artist.

The entire project was based around the production and promotion
of a CD and DVD, therefore the majority of income would come
from product sales, label share of PPL royalties and secondary
licensing only – live income, publishing and artist performance
royalties (the artist's share of PPL and PRS)[1] were not included. The
sort of expenses they included in the project costs were: a project
manager fee of around 10 per cent, accountancy costs, legal fees,
tour support for a small UK promotional tour, the costs of recording
an album and filming a tour DVD, manufacturing costs, showcases,
radio promotion and full marketing support (including print and
online PR, marketing costs and a marketing manager), the cost of
musicians, and a budget for expenses at festivals.

The budget formed part of a presentation of approximately five
pages (plus pictures) that covered:

• who the artist was

• the product that was going to be created – in this case, a CD
and DVD

• what content would be included

• the look and feel of the product

• the technical specs of what would be needed to produce the recording and film

• a production plan for shooting the DVD.

DOING THE DEAL

Once the proposal had been accepted, contracts were negotiated with the investment fund. These covered:

• a licence for the IP of the idea of the album and DVD

• a recording agreement

• a product development, production services and licensing contract

• override options, and

• an assignment of royalties.

Although these were standardised contracts provided by the funder, they did not originate from the music industry. Harvey-Piper asked her music lawyer to vet the contract; an essential part of the process was accessing legal advice from a lawyer who was familiar with investor agreements, and who could make sure that they were appropriate for a music deal.

This process was fairly quick; the first meeting took place mid-September, with the deal completed at the end of November. The money was released from the fund in four stages, to be made available at specific dates that were predetermined by the structure of the fund.

After the project had started, Harvey-Piper was required to provide monthly reporting on progress and spending for six months, and meet with the funder every two months to evidence the outcome of each tranche of funding.

Overall, she has learnt a lot from the experience, and, as she explained, it has worked well in her case:

> "If the opportunity came up, I would absolutely do it again. We've had a really good experience. I talked to other people who'd gone halfway through the experience: it didn't work out for them, for various reasons, and that's very disappointing.
>
> If someone says 'we love the music and we want to put some money into it', what's not to like? Provided that you understand what you're signing away, and you're prepared to do that … in the end you have to go with what the artist wants to do."

KERRY HARVEY-PIPER'S TIPS ON WORKING WITH AN INVESTOR AND PRODUCING A BUDGET

1. Take the process seriously

2. Don't be afraid to ask the obvious or explore the 'what ifs' to make sure you understand the deal

3. Make sure you have a good lawyer who is used to these sorts of deals

4. Be prepared for it to take longer than you might expect, or for it to fall through

6. Do check you understand your budgets, have a good accountant and can work a spreadsheet

7. Be realistic about the costs – don't underestimate, or overinflate

8. Build-in a contingency for unexpected costs, especially with touring

9. Ensure you have a good, well thought-through plan, and a team of people you can rely on and with whom you really want to work

WHAT IS INVESTMENT?

Investment normally refers to money from funders who will buy shares in your company (also known as equity) in return for financial benefits. These benefits might be in the form of either:

• Dividends, which are a share of your profits shareholders expect you to pay them on an annual basis; or,

• Share value increases, in which, due to your company doing well in the long run, investors can see an opportunity to make money in the future by selling their shares for substantially more than they paid for them. Investors may choose to put in some of their investment as a loan rather than in return for equity.

If you are only looking for modest amounts of money to set up a small label, for example, you might be able to get a friend to invest money in return for a proportion of the profit.Or perhaps another, larger label might want to give you some money to start up in return for a share of your company.

It might be necessary to go to a private equity fund to secure investment into your business. The money in private equity funds typically comes either from wealthy individuals investing into a specialist fund, or from 'institutional investors' such as pension funds, insurance companies and banks, who have access to huge amounts of money to invest.

On balance, it is highly likely that many who are successful in obtaining investment will secure it from a private individual or another music-based company. However it's still helpful to understand some technical terms for the different ways investments are made, because they are used by investors, and it will help to be able to speak their language if you want to work with them. Author Stephen Bloomfield[2] defines four types of venture capital investment as seed capital, venture money, private equity and mezzanine finance.

1. Seed Capital

Money that is used to start the business or project – this sometimes comes from funds but mainly from your own money or from friends, family, or other private individuals.

2. Venture Money

The type of investment money associated with 'angel' investors and specialist firms in which money is put into early-stage businesses that have shown evidence of promise beyond seed capital stage.

3. Private Equity

A term that is sometimes used interchangeably with venture money, but specifically means money that: comes from larger institutional investors… usually invested into well established businesses beyond the stage of product development – to take a developing business to the next level before flotation.

Flotation means selling shares to the public on the stock exchange, becoming a public limited company (PLC.) instead of a limited company (LTD.), that can't be sold on the stock exchange.

Unsurprisingly, companies that achieve this will be substantial in size.

4. Mezzanine Finance

This is worth defining, just to complete the set, but won't be relevant to many readers of this guide. It is a specialist branch of lending that mixes the characteristics of a loan with equity, and tends to be used in the short term to bridge a gap in funding.

This guide is focused on small companies, therefore will only look at the first two types of investment which present higher risks for potential investors than investing in shares in a more established company. To compensate, there are some tax reliefs available to individuals in order to incentivise small businesses investment.

TAX INCENTIVES FOR INVESTORS

Tax relief vehicles that are made available by the Government effectively reduce the cost of making an investment and reduce the risk to the investor's money. The main schemes available to investors in individual companies are the Enterprise Investment Scheme (EIS) and the Seed Enterprise Investment Scheme (SEIS)[3].

Some will use collective investment schemes such as EIS funds or venture capital trusts, which in turn will invest in several different companies. Investors can also use their investments as a way to shelter their money from Capital Gains Tax and Inheritance Tax, using appropriate HMRC tax reliefs such as Business Property Relief and (in certain limited circumstances), Sideways Loss Relief[4]. The most important thing for music companies to understand is whether or not they might be eligible for one or other of these schemes.

1. Enterprise Investment Scheme

The EIS is designed to help smaller, higher risk trading companies raise finance by offering a range of tax reliefs to investors who purchase new shares in those companies. This policy was introduced because the Government actively wants investors to support these smaller, high-risk companies, whom they know cannot easily obtain finance from the banks or large-scale investors.

This scheme operates as a tax incentive for the investors, in the form of a deduction from their tax bill that is equal to a percentage of the money that they have used to buy the shares.

The tax relief available with the EIS is (at the time or writing) 30 per cent of the cost of the shares, to be set against the investor's income tax liability for the tax year in which the investment was made; in other words, investors get 30 per cent of what they spend on purchasing shares deducted from their income before tax. They have to hold on to the shares for three years and can use the scheme to invest directly in a 'qualifying company', or in a fund that then goes on to invest on their behalf into multiple 'qualifying companies'. Companies with assets under £15 million and fewer than 250 employees that's almost certainly everyone reading this guide – qualify for the EIS.

An important point for music companies is that the EIS can't be used to invest in buying existing copyrights nor collecting royalties from them, although companies that will be originating their own copyrights should qualify. This brings about a particular problem for music publishing companies. Because works are created by songwriters and composers and the copyright in them is assigned to a publishing company, publishers can be caught out by this restriction. Specialist advice should be taken if publishing rights are going to be part of a potential EIS qualifying investment.

Also, the shareholder/investor cannot be already related to the business, preventing EIS from being used to invest in your own company, or take investment from certain close family members, current directors/shareholders or others who are already closely associated with, or connected to, the company.

2. Seed Enterprise Investment Scheme

SEIS differs from EIS in that it is specifically focused on small start-up or early-stage companies (i.e. trading for under two years, with fewer than 25 employees, whose assets are worth less than £200,000 and have not been part of any similar scheme previously). Investors can invest up to a maximum of £100,000 each year into SEIS- qualifying companies and gain tax relief of 50 per cent of their investment against their next Income Tax bill, a greater incentive than the normal EIS. If they are a Capital Gains Tax payer, they will also qualify for 28 per cent tax relief against their Capital Gains Tax bill. As well as providing a potential upfront tax break of up to 78 per cent, if the investment increases in value, the gains will be exempt from Capital Gains Tax. If it falls in value, the investor can offset the loss against their income, further reducing the cost to the investor. Companies can raise up to £150,000 in total via SEIS. As with EIS, the investors have to hold the shares for three years[5].

This reflects the greater risk taken by investors of a start-up company versus the 30 per cent Income Tax relief for investors in more established EIS ventures, and makes it a great opportunity for the music industry to get investment.

An example of an independent company's attempt to build a channel for investment in new music is the Music Managers Forum (MMF) launch in early 2013 of Amplify Music SEIS Opportunities; a collaborative venture with Amp Channel Music Limited whose managing director, Tom Bywater, launched the Power Amp Music EIS Fund in 2008.

Brian Message, Chairman of the MMF, explained that the MMF would be involved in all aspects of artist selection, deal negotiation and artist development. At the time of writing they had their first deal near to launch, but they hope to develop a string of deals in the future that will help interested private investors find strong artists with professional management in whom they can invest, within an SEIS-qualifying company that mitigates some of their risks. The company will also spread the costs of getting the documentation drawn up for investors across a number of qualifying companies, making the deals more viable to complete. Amplify Music favours working with experienced management teams who will be able to make a profit from the investment in the artist.

3. Venture Capital Trust

The VCT scheme is designed to encourage individuals to invest indirectly in a range of small higher-risk trading companies whose shares and securities are not listed on a recognised stock exchange. VCTs are similar to investment trusts. They are run by fund managers who are usually members of larger investment groups. Investors can subscribe for, or buy, shares in a VCT, which invests in trading companies, providing them with funds to help them develop and grow.

VCTs offer a range of attractive tax reliefs. On the way in, investments attract income tax relief of 30%, meaning £1,000 worth of shares effectively costs the investor just £700, while on the way out, both dividends and capital gains are tax-free.

David Glick, founder of Edge Investments, which offers both VCT and EIS investments, cautions against what he is concerned may be a general view across the industry – that the tax breaks available for EIS and VCT investments mean that investors somehow won't want to make their money back, or that they are a 'soft option' for companies looking to raise capital. He says:

> "The gains are indeed tax free, but people in the music and other creative industries sometimes fail to understand that the tax break is not for them, the tax break is for the investor, and if they try and get their hands on it, the investor will go elsewhere."

Further discussing the restrictions on acquired IP and licensing-based businesses which can affect music companies as mentioned earlier, David Glick explains:

> "With a VCT, there's a 20 per cent acquired IP test. It's a real impediment, namely that we cannot invest in any business at any time that makes more than 20 per cent of its income, at any time, from IP that it has acquired. This is potentially a problem for growing publishing companies, for instance, which often acquire some copyrights when they commence operations in order to generate the cash to help them sign newer writers. It could mean that to begin with, for instance, a start-up publishing company generates 100 per cent of its income from acquired IP. A VCT could not invest in such a company."

WHERE CAN MUSIC COMPANIES FIND INVESTORS?

If you are a music company, and you want an investor, where can you actually go to find one? There are three likely sources: investment management firms, angel investors and angel networks and people in your own network.

1. Investment Management Firms (Venture Capital)

There are a handful of investment management firms that specialise in raising venture capital to invest in the media sector, of which music forms a part. This section will focus on three specifically - Ingenious Media, Edge Investments and Icebreaker.

Ingenious Media

The largest of these is Ingenious Media, which has been operating since 1998 and describes itself as "an investment and advisory group". The firm is known as the largest media investment firm in Europe, claiming to have raised over £8 billion from investors to put into that sector. The most relevant of its four arms, for our purposes, is Ingenious Ventures, which is the private equity division of the company – the one that decides on where to invest the money raised from its numerous funds. For example, the company currently offers investors the opportunity to put their money into Ingenious Entertainment VCT, just one of a number of funds that the firm offers, which will invest it in live music and events companies.

However, it is important to understand that Ingenious does not currently invest in creating new music content, having left that market several years ago. It does invest in live music, and also in creating new content in film, television and computer games. In 2012, in written evidence to the BIS Parliamentary Select Committee enquiry Support for the Creative Economy, Ingenious stated:

> "We have previously invested in recorded music, including albums by Peter Gabriel and The Prodigy (a number one hit album), but we now focus on music festivals and other live events."

So, while in the past Ingenious did invest in music content, with partners such as Cooking Vinyl, Real World Records and Independiente, they are now focusing on live music, with investments in major events like Liverpool Sound City, Creamfields, Rewind Festival, Apple Cart Festival, Field Day Festival and Brighton's Shakedown Festival. They estimate that their investment into music has been around £30m over the last three years.[6]

I spoke to Patrick Bradley, the CEO of Ingenious Ventures about why this change from recorded to live music investments came about. While the investments in recordings were successful, and attractive to investors because of the tax break offered by the venture capital trust structure and EIS scheme, the growth of the live music market over the same time period made it a much more profitable investment proposition. Bradley says:

"We had made investments in three different areas of music – a music fund for recorded music, Stage Three Music, which we'd created [publishing], and live events. We'd been long-term investors in Cream, but then we started to invest in festivals such as Eighties Rewind and so on. We realised that you can't pirate live events, for which there was a great demand, and artists liked it because they got paid. There was [massive] growth in that sector over the last five years, and that's where the value was. We knew that buyers would be looking to buy successful festivals, so our focus moved to this and away from the recording and the music publishing sectors."

Helpfully, Ingenious publishes information on its website about all of its funds and how to apply for funding. In the first instance, it advises companies looking for investment to contact the investment division directly with an email to the CEO of Ingenious Ventures. This email message should include a brief account of your investment requirements, the amount you want to raise, the type of company structure envisaged, together with other basic background information about you and your company.

Ingenious is very 'hands-on' and will normally look to take a significant share of your business and a seat on your board in order to safeguard its investment, ensuring the presence of the expertise required to assist the company's growth. It is easy to see from this that it is only likely to be a tiny percentage of music companies who will be able to meet the requirements of an investor like Ingenious Media.

Overall it is estimated that less than one per cent of approaches that are made to Ingenious Ventures by companies looking for investment result in an investment being made, because they are unsuitable in one way or other. In the live music sector, the focus has been on both existing and new festivals, but still with a high proportion of submissions being rejected. Patrick Bradley confirmed:

"The policy of Ingenious Ventures is to meet as many management teams as possible, unless the propositions are excluded for being totally unsuitable or outside the criteria of funds available. However for very early stage submissions, the proportion of meetings will be much lower (around 10 per cent) with later stage propositions more likely to result in a meeting around 50 per cent). Ingenious also tracks management teams that interest them, who may be too early on or not quite meet investment criteria, by holding a meeting to establish a dialogue which may come to fruition as the proposition develops over time."

Edge Investments

Edge Investments, a specialist fund manager focused on the creative industries is another well-known name in music investment. It was founded in 2005 by former entertainment lawyer David Glick, and has raised more than £145 million from investors. Edge's main fund is the Edge Performance Venture Capital Trust, which has raised almost £125 million since its launch in 2006, which, it claims, makes it the largest VCT in the UK. As with Ingenious Media, Edge looks for businesses run by experienced executives, and ideally for developed companies that are already profitable. Outlining Edge's investment criteria, David Glick says it looks for companies that:

• are real businesses – not just ideas – typically (but not always) with a million pounds of turnover[7].

• have an able management team.

• are capable of tripling the investment over five years, and allowing investors to exit within seven years.

• are in the creative industries.

• have a strong business plan.

• allow Edge to take a minority shareholding

– VCT rules prevent the firm from owning a majority stake in the businesses it invests in.

Edge has made a series of investments into events promotions businesses. For example, it has invested in the businesses of promoters of tours by the likes of Bon Jovi and Elbow. David Glick says:

"We have put about £60m to work and put on around 300 shows in the past couple of years. That must make us one of the largest investors in the UK live music sector."

So both Edge Performance VCT and the range of Ingenious funds are investing in music, but mainly in live music. Of course, some of this money will trickle down to smaller companies through festival income, music licensing fees and so on. Edge has a track record of investing in music-related technology companies, but like Ingenious it is not currently investing in individual recorded music projects or in record labels.

Icebreaker

A third big name in music investment is the Icebreaker Fund, which still invests in recorded music. The investment vehicle used here is different from Edge's and Ingenious' use of VCTs and EIS funds. Icebreaker sets up LLPs (limited liability partnerships) as a way for investors to invest their own and borrowed money into a partnership, which then invests in music and tech ventures.

Icebreaker proudly claims that:

"Since 2004, the LLPs have assisted in the production and distribution of nearly 150 music albums from a range of established and aspiring British and other artists and musicians."

Icebreaker is well known for investing in artists such as Beverley Knight and Ali Campbell, and more recently Sinead O'Connor, Marilyn Manson and The Cranberries. It has also invested in less well-known artists. For example, in 2011 Icebreaker invested in singer Jake Morley. A case study on Jake Morley and Icebreaker is included earlier in this chapter.

It's good to know that there is some investment going into music, however it is important to understand that accessing it requires a totally different approach to applying for a grant, say, where the process is meant to be fair and equal. Only a tiny proportion of companies that contact the kind of investment firms described in this chapter will ever get a meeting, let alone receive funding. It is thought to be around 5 per cent of approaches that get through to the meeting stage, with fewer than 1 per cent ever getting funded. This contrasts with an estimated 30 per cent success rate of first-time applicants for Arts Council Grants, and the 10 per cent success rate of applicants for PRS for Music's British Music Abroad Scheme.

In recent years, investment management companies in all sectors have all had to defend themselves from negative commentary on their tax arrangements and sales methods. For example, Icebreaker received a critical judgement concerning one of its schemes in a tribunal between itself and HMRC[8]. The main criticism of investment firms is that the Government has provided a tax incentive for investors to encourage them to put money into small firms (the EIS, Seed EIS and VCT structures), yet some investment companies use the incentives more as a way to help wealthy individuals and corporate clients to legally limit their tax liabilities, than as a vehicle to provide investment opportunities in small businesses[9].

Investment companies have argued that they are using the schemes for their intended purpose of funding the smaller, more risky investments that cannot get finance through other means. Some firms (across the investment world, not specifically those mentioned here) have been accused of marketing to unsophisticated investors who are putting money into the funds that they could not afford to lose should the companies fail to make a return on the investment.

These operators have tried to reassure both government and investors by emphasising their experience in, and close ties to, the media sector. Ingenious, for instance, does this by showing that it is risking the firm's own money on the investments. Like Edge Investments, it has also made efforts to get its funds and VCT's pre-approved by HMRC to ensure that they do comply with regulations. In the end, though, all of the investment firms mentioned in this book are providing money that is going into the music sector, and have, they say, the very difficult job of convincing investors and their financial advisers to put any money at all into what many people regard as a fickle and risky sector.

In spite of these criticisms, it's clear that investment firms have made a real contribution to the finance mix available to the music industry. Martin Goldschmidt, owner of established independent record label Cooking Vinyl, has done deals with both Ingenious Media (signing the band The Prodigy) and Icebreaker (signing artists and groups including Marilyn Manson, The Cult and The Cranberries, the Orb and The Subways). If he had been using only the company's own money, he would have been in the position of taking on all of the risk of the deals alone, but working with investors allowed him to make investments in these artists without overextending his company. With both deals, Goldschmidt says:

> "It de-risks the deal. We would have done the same deals anyway – not all, but all the big ones anyway… and our margin would be pretty much the same. In this way, there's no risk in it for us."

2. Angel Investors And Angel Networks (Seed Money And Venture Capital)

Business Angels are like those individuals we see on programmes like BBC2's Dragon's Den. They are normally experienced business people who have made money and want to invest their cash and expertise in other promising businesses. The name 'angels' comes from the theatre world, whose investors in new shows traditionally represented a softer type of investor than today's business angels. The UK Business Angels Association estimates that there are 18,000 or so individual business angels in the UK, many of them operating as part of angel networks that developed to bring investors together with businesses looking for funding[10]. For example, the organisation London Business Angels holds regular events where selected businesses can pitch to their network of angels. They say that they receive around 1,000 applications per year, and put only 40–50 forward to pitch to investors – meaning about 95 per cent of applications are rejected[11].

Applications must meet criteria similar to those for investment firms – they must come from companies that have high growth potential; that is, they must have the potential to be a market leader, to increase their value many times over with a product or service that offers a 'high barrier to entry'. This means that your company is selling something patentable or possesses some other advantage that will stop its business idea being easily copied. Some angel networks will charge businesses a few hundred pounds to review your application and help them to prepare to pitch to the network.

Jenny Tooth, CEO of the UK Business Angels Association confirmed that most angels would not specifically look to invest into music, in fact even the term 'creative industries' is not one that they would tend to use. She said: 'Angel investors generally have a range of perceptions and misconceptions around creative industries entrepreneurs that affects their willingness and approach to investing … however all angel networks are investing widely in digital media and content.'[12]

Some of the characteristics that both investment companies and Angel investors will be looking for in the firms that they invest in are:

• experienced entrepreneurial management with a demonstrable track record of commercial success

• a capacity for international expansion

• high growth potential (at least 15 per cent per year for a number of years)

• scalability of earnings (that the company has a structure and product that will allow it to multiply its turnover)

• a business looking for between £250,000 and £2m of growth capital

• explicit proof of a viable business concept already delivering revenues and/or credible evidence of consumer traction

• a business that is not a pure start-up, i.e. one that has already started trading.

All of the examples cited in these first two sections represent relatively tough investment propositions. Things may be a bit different when it comes to private individuals who are in your existing network, who are likely to be more flexible in their requirements for growth and who may be willing to invest at a more modest level.

3. Investment From Your Own Networks (Seed Money)

You don't have to go through an Angel network to find an investor. You can use your own network. Put the word out that you are looking for investment – there may be companies or individuals, people you know or have worked with – who might want to put money into your business. Davin McDermott of management consultancy Create Tech advises:

> "Approaching anyone cold is just very hard and the odds are stacked against you, I think going through your network is the key … every meeting you have is going to be worthwhile: all of it is preparation for the one meeting where someone is ready to put their hand in their pocket. If you've talked to many people and they've raised various issues, that has made you look at them and focus on them, that can only prepare you for the right investor."

That was certainly the experience of Sam McGregor. He failed to get money from a series of banks, but he put the word out to people in his own social networks that he was looking for an investor, as detailed in case study G.

Music industry lawyer Berkeley Edwards says that he is seeing an increasing number of new artists who are winning investment directly through their own networks. He says:

> "The examples that I've seen generally have a manager involved who can say to the investor, 'you're not just chucking £100,000 at a 22-year-old musician … this is the business plan we've got over the next 18 months'. If you've got a business plan and a strategy, it looks a lot more attractive, and I think a proactive manager who's got a track record of doing things independently is an incredible asset for an artist. It provides peace of mind for the investor, bearing in mind that the majority of these investors aren't expecting to see a [massive] return on their cash, they're just wanting to invest in the arts."

So these investors are coming in at a lower level, with anything between £5,000 and £100,000 of investment for small firms, hoping to make profits, but willing to take more of a risk than angels or VC firms and perhaps deriving a major part of their satisfaction from being close to artistic talent.

Wherever you find your investor, you should take this process very seriously.

Martin Goldschmidt of Cooking Vinyl advises:

> "You're trying to persuade people to invest their money in you. So you've got to persuade them that you've got the right product, that for some reason your artist is the one they should be backing, that you've got the right market experience to deliver that, and that you've got the right business experience to do the backend – the accounting, everything like that, right? And make them a profit …"

> "So you need to go to them with a really professional business proposal. It has got to be compelling, it has got to look professional, the numbers have got to make sense, and if you lie they'll probably smell it – people just do. I think you should believe in it. You've got to put together a proposal that, [if the situation were reversed, and someone came to you for money] you'd invest in. You've got to put yourself in their shoes."

KEY MUSIC AND MEDIA INVESTMENT ORGANISATIONS

Ingenious Media

Investment and advisory group well known for their investment in media and entertainment companies.

Edge Investments

Specialist fund manager for the creative industries.

Icebreaker

Investment fund management firm specialising in entertainment.

London Business Angels

Angel investment network that helps high-growth, early stage companies raise £100,000–£1m.

Angel Investment Network

Internet platform introducing investors to entrepreneurs.

Crowdcube

Online equity investment platform mixing crowdfunding with investment.

Seedrs.Com

Allows online investing into new start-up and seed stage businesses.

MeWe360

Not-for-profit development house for creative entrepreneurs including a subsidised incubator. An incubator is an organisation that provides members with access to advice and support to help them become investment ready, and also has a commercial investment arm to invest in the best of its members' businesses.

Capital For Enterprise

Fund management company connected to the Government which will be integrated into the Government's new Business Bank portfolio of services. Active programmes include the UK Innovation

Investment Fund, the Enterprise Capital Fund Programme, and the
Aspire Fund (for women-led businesses).

NINE

Conclusion

The title of this book – Easy Money? – is purposefully ironic. The question mark indicates that, although there clearly is money out there, it takes confidence, knowledge and skill to get your hands on it.

My approach to writing this book was influenced by the DIY ethos; the belief that musicians and small music companies can deal in a global music market, given the right product, information and funding.

The objectives of this book, then, were to provide a valuable reference for the thousands of companies and musicians that would otherwise have to research available funding themselves, and to avoid a lack of information being the cause of good projects going unsupported. I have tried to read as widely as possible about what is available, weed out the irrelevant and focus on giving a realistic picture of the chances of accessing money. I am very grateful to the scores of funders, musicians and music companies who kindly shared their direct experience with me, and consequently with all the readers of this book.

The rest of this chapter sets out why funding from outside the music industry has increased in relevance to small music companies and musicians, and reflects on the challenges inherent in taking responsibility for raising funding.

HOW INTRA-INDUSTRY FUNDING HAS CHANGED OVER TIME

There has always been a strong intra-industry funding model, as detailed in the Introduction, whereby deals are made between music industry businesses that help to cash flow music production and artist development. In 2013, record labels remain the largest investor in new music by a wide margin[1], and the aspiration of many artists and small companies will still be to secure funding from a corporate partner, but the diversity of companies within the industry that can provide such significant deals is not what it was. As a result, artists, musicians, songwriters, composers and small companies are now taking much greater responsibility for the funding of music than they did in previous decades.

From the late 1950s to the early 1970s in the UK, large record companies controlled the recording, distribution and marketing of music. They, along with the large publishers and promoters, held the financial resources, and consequently were in a position to dictate the terms of artist contracts. Artists were supplicants to companies who had access to the expensive recording equipment needed to make records, and physical distribution and radio were mostly inaccessible to smaller players. There are many stories of artists of that era who were poorly treated by their commercial partners.

Rock biographies set in the 1950s–1970s frequently feature stories about artists getting ripped off, and also chart the subsequent rise of savvy artist managers who were more effective at fighting the artists' corner. There are, of course, plenty of tales of artists enjoying record company largesse, before walking away having never recouped the investment made in them.

The mid-1970s to the early 1990s witnessed a period of rapid growth of independent UK labels, whose financial situation was often precarious, and who succeeded in part because of support from major labels[2].

From the late 1990s onwards, there was a consolidation of major record labels and large independents into a small number of global corporations. Digital and technological advances over the same period saw a renaissance of small independent labels, many of which were owned by artists who were able to make use of cheaper recording technology and access digital distribution and marketing tools in order to reach an audience. These new artist-owned companies included a number of artists that had either abandoned or been dropped by their previous labels, Simply Red being one such example. While there are a number of artists who owned their own recordings and publishing rights in the 1970s and 1980s, they were pioneers who were atypical for the time.

INDEPENDENT FUNDING IS THE NEW NORMAL

We have entered a period defined by a number of new factors: generally speaking, artist advances are more meagre than ever; major music corporations struggle to consistently provide value to shareholders; and artists are more empowered than ever.

Artists are able to inform themselves about music and recording technology, finance, the law, marketing and distribution, and, more than ever, are contributing to such complex debates as piracy and streaming remuneration. Media and music industry discussions often frame these developments as being either wholly positive or negative.

The positive view is that artists are more in control of their own careers, meaning that relationships with intermediaries have changed from dependencies to partnerships.

Examples of this range from Radiohead's *In Rainbows* album campaign, to self-made Internet stars such as Alex Day. Champions of this trend include crowdfunding superstar Amanda Palmer and musician-turned-global business mogul Jay-Z.

The counter view is more negative: that established music industry companies are not investing in and developing new artists from as early a stage and in as great a quantity as before. This supposedly results in more of a buyer's market, whereby artists are forced to fund their own development until a commercial partner can be found: in effect, plumping themselves up for sale by shouldering all of the early financial risk and doing all of the foundation building.

Both these views, as reported by the media and assumed by some in the music industry, are over-simplifications of how the music industry has changed in recent years.

It is my firm belief that artists in the 21st century have to, and should, take greater responsibility for their careers by educating themselves about business, finance and the law.

They don't have to do this alone; there is an array of specialist support available, and it is the aim of this book to identify to musicians and music businesses how they can access finance.

There are, naturally, certain demands that come with funding. There is always a trade-off between the funder and the person receiving the funding. In the intra-industry funding model (mentioned earlier), this is well understood. For example, in the relationship between a record label and an artist, the artist gives up a certain amount of control over their rights and how their music is managed in return for the investment and expertise they receive from the label.

Our challenge, then, if we are looking for other sources of funding, is to spend as much effort on understanding and learning the language of funding as we do on our relationships within the music industry. We need to know what it takes to attract money, what you are expected to deliver, the motivations of the different funders and how they are aligned (or clashing) with the motivations of the artist.

In the future, the music industry will need to be fluent in funder-speak. It will be the language that maintains a diverse range of entry points for new music to get money – easy or otherwise.

TEN

Additional Trusts and Foundations

The Directory of Grant Making Trusts 22nd Edition 2012/13 lists 44 trusts that give money to music. These will be especially relevant if you are a classical musician or composer, or doing work that has a social or educational purpose, but there are trusts that cover specifically performing arts, arts from specific cultures, disability arts, community arts, access to the arts and arts management policy and planning.

Angus Allnatt Charitable Foundation

Grants for third sector organisations (TSOs) undertaking music and recreation projects for young people in the UK.

The Hervey Benham Charitable Trust

For those living in Colchester or north east Essex, who have exceptional artistic talent (especially in music), and are disadvantaged in a way which affects their development.

. . .

The Britten-Pears Foundation

BPF exists to ensure that the legacy of Benjamin Britten and Peter Pears continues to be enjoyed worldwide. In addition to supporting Aldeburgh Music with an annual £250,000 grants, it operates three open grant schemes.

1. The Britten awards support performances of Britten works around the world, especially those with an audience-development aspect;

2. BPF commissions support the writing of new works by British and British-based composers;

3. Local community grants support projects within a 20 mile radius of Aldeburgh.

BBC Performing Arts Fund

Established in 2003, it has awarded a total of £4 million in grants over the last 10 years. Each year the Fund's work focuses on a different art form, most recently theatre (2013) and music (2012). Grants are distributed via two schemes, one for individuals and one for community groups, who, for reasons of lack of existing support, personal background or circumstance, need the fund's help to reach their potential.

The Derek Butler Trust

The charity currently makes grants available for music and music education.

CJ Cadbury Charitable Trust

Projects including music and arts.

.   .   .

The Cross Trust

Enables young Scots in all fields in need of financial support to fulfil their potential.

The Deakin Charitable Trust

No website specifically dedicated to this fund. For people studying music and who live in the immediate Woking area.

The Delius Trust

The Trust promotes the music of Frederick Delius and of British composers born since 1860, by giving help towards the cost of performances, publications and recordings. In addition, assistance is occasionally offered to organisations and institutions active in this field. Priority is always given to the promotion of the works of Delius, especially those that are rarely performed.

Dunard Fund

No website specifically dedicated to this fund. Funds training in classical music.

Esmee Fairbairn Foundation

Large foundation that gave almost £8 million to the arts in 2012 including many music organisations.

The Family Rich Charities Trust

No website specifically dedicated to this fund. Funds art and music therapy.

The Joyce Fletcher Charitable Trust

Funds art and music related to therapy or welfare, particularly in South West England.

Gerald Finzi Charitable Trust

Awards scholarships to give opportunities for broadening horizons or taking a new path. Their focus is arts-based in the widest sense, but proposals must have a musical foundation.

The John Feeney Charitable Trust

Awards small grants to arts organisations in the Birmingham area.

The Hugh Fraser Foundation

No website specifically dedicated to this fund. Tends to award grants to charitable bodies to assist with their work. Grants are often made in successive years in order to maintain their momentum and effectiveness. Grants favour West Scotland but all applicants from Scotland are welcomed.

The Freshgate Trust Foundation

No website specifically dedicated to this fund. Awards grants to local organisations for charitable causes across a broad range of purposes including education (including travel and training) and music. Prioritises organisations within Sheffield & South Yorkshire.

The Gatsby Charitable Foundation

Gatsby will continue to support the arts organisations and initiatives it has built long relationships with, while occasionally funding new projects in harmony with the Trustees' passions and aims.

The Harding Trust

No website specifically dedicated to this fund. Liverpool focus – charitable objectives include the development and maintenance of public education in, and appreciation of, the art and science of music. Support comes in the form of sponsoring or by otherwise supporting public concerts, recitals and performances by amateur and professional organisations.

The Hinrichsen Foundation

Devoted to the promotion of music. Their main focus is assisting contemporary composition and its performance, and musical research.

The Holst Foundation

A grant giving charity whose funds are directed primarily towards the performance of music by living composers. The majority of grants are awarded to performing groups; individuals can usually only be supported if an application is made on their behalf by performers or promoters.

The Kathleen Trust

No website specifically dedicated to this fund. The trust offers loans to buy instruments and equipment and bursaries to pay course fees.

The Leche Trust

Offers assistance to academic, educational or other organisations concerned with music, drama, dance and the arts.

The Mackintosh Foundation

No website specifically dedicated to this fund. The majority of funding is given to projects in the UK in support of theatre and the performing arts.

The MacRobert Trust

Applications are invited from across the UK. Preference is given to organisations based in Scotland that encourage young people to take an interest in music and the performing arts, including charitable companies which encourage participation in youth orchestras, youth opera and other theatrical performance.

WM Mann Foundation

No website specifically dedicated to this fund. Support for charitable activities in Scotland but has a preference for projects that benefit young people and for arts related projects. Preference is also given to smaller local charities headquartered and/or active in the Glasgow area. The Trustees prefer one-off support for special projects.

Sir George Martin Trust

Provides funding to charitable projects in West and North Yorkshire. Considers applications for the capital needs of theatres. Also considers projects in areas which are known to have been of definite interest to Sir George Martin during his lifetime.

The Mayfield Valley Arts Trust

No website specifically dedicated to this fund. Committed to helping young artists of recognised potential, and offering them a platform/audience, which otherwise they would have difficulty achieving.

The Peter Moores Foundation

The foundation gives particular focus to the fields of operatic music, the visual arts and education.

The Oakdale Trust

The Oakdale Trust provides funding for charities and voluntary bodies working in Wales on social and community projects.

The Ouseley Trust

The Ouseley Trust was set up to promote and maintain to a high standard the choral services of the Church of England, the Church in Wales and the Church of Ireland.

It does this by making grants to cathedrals, choral foundations, parish churches, choir schools and other relevant institutions.

The Pallant Charitable Trust

No website specifically dedicated to this fund. The Trustees' objective is to promote mainstream church music both in choral and instrumental form.

PRS Members Benevolent Fund

Fund to help songwriters and composers who experience ill health or financial hardship.

The RVW Trust

The RVW Trust is one of the most significant sources in the UK of funding for contemporary and recent British music. The trust's principal areas of grant considerations are: British composers; assistance re performance and recordings; national organisations who promote public knowledge and appreciation of 20th and 21st century British music; occasional support for educational projects; support for post-graduate students of composition taking first masters degrees at British institutions.

The Radcliffe Trust

The Radcliffe Trust supports classical music performance and training especially chamber music, composition and music education.

The Rhondda Cynon Taff (Welsh Church Acts Fund)

No website specifically dedicated to this fund. The Welsh Church Act Fund grant scheme is available to voluntary and community groups operating in Rhondda Cynon Taff, Merthyr and Bridgend. Applications to the fund are invited from Churches, Chapels, Community Organisations and Charities.

The Rowlands Trust

No website specifically dedicated to this fund. Grants are available to local registered charities in the arts and culture field for charitable activities that benefit residents of Tyne & Wear, Northumberland, County Durham and Teesside.

Miss S M Tutton Charitable Trust

No website specifically dedicated to this fund. Trustees allocate financial assistance for young opera singers, principally through the Sybil Tutton awards, and through grants and donations to organisations involved in training these young artists. The aim in all cases is to facilitate the development of artistic excellence.

The Whitaker Charitable Trust

No website specifically dedicated to this fund. Available to Third Sector Organisations in Nottinghamshire. In particular, the scheme wishes to support: local charities; Scottish charities and music education.

The Winston Churchill Memorial Trust

Annual fellowship for travel for an original research purpose in the arts.

. . .

Youth Music Programme

Charity funding music programmes with children and young people.

ELEVEN

Terms and Conditions

Terms And Conditions

The information contained in this publication has been extensively checked for accuracy and was technically and factually correct at time of going to press (August 2013).

Funding and tax regimes change over time and funding schemes come and go and the advice and strategies contained herein may not be suitable for your own situation. For these reasons, this guide should not be considered or interpreted as a substitute for independent professional advice. Neither publisher, author or contributors are liable for any direct or indirect consequences arising from decisions or actions carried out as a consequence of reading or acting upon the contents of this publication.

Similarly, all external links to websites and other additional sources of information were correct and accessible at time of publication.

The contents of these external sources may change over time, become unavailable, irrelevant or out of date, for which this guide's publisher and author are not responsible.

End notes have been added to the text, wherever I was aware of a change of name for a fund or funder.

Endnotes

How to Use This Guide

1. Creative and Cultural Industries Music Statistics, compiled 2012/13 by Creative and Cultural Skills using 2009 data on business size. 81 per cent of music businesses employ 1–4 people; a further 17 per cent employ between 5 and 50 people.
2. UK Government defines micro-businesses as employing between 1 and 10 people, small businesses as those employing up to 50 people, and medium-sized business employing between 50 to 250 people.

1. Introduction

1. **www.musictank.co.uk/resources/reports/wadsworth-remake-remodel**
   (accessed 02.08.13)
2. A reference to the 1929 US Stock Market crash, widely considered to be the biggest economic disaster in history, triggering the Great Depression of the 1930s.
3. *Venture Capital Funding, A Practical Guide To Raising Finance*, 2nd Edition, Stephen Bloomfield, Kogan Page (2008)
4. In his book *Popular Music and the State in the UK* (2007), Martin Cloonan argues that the Labour party courted the music industry in the 1990s, and that "by the time of the 1997 election, the political establishment was familiar with leading recording industry personnel". He cites a speech in 1997 by the first DCMS Secretary of State Chris Smith, who said: "The new British Government wants to do all it can to create the right environment for the music business to flourish."
5. *Banking On A Hit: The Funding Dilemma For Britain's Music Businesses.* DCMS (2001)
   http://www.docstoc.com/docs/29486179/Banking-on-a-hit
   (accessed 18.08.13)
6. Definitions of what an SME is not standardised across the EU, nor is there a single definition of a small firm, mainly because of the wide diversity of businesses. Broadly speaking it's a category of companies whose turnover does not exceed £11.2 million and employs fewer than 250 people. More on this here:
   https://webarchive.nationalarchives.gov.uk/+/http://www.dti.gov.uk/SME4/define.htm
   (accessed 18.08.13)
7. *SME Music Businesses: Business Growth and Access To Finance*, DCMS (2006)

8. *Music Money Map*, DCMS (last updated 2010)

9. The EFG is a scheme allowing companies with viable business plans but who narrowly fail to obtain a loan, particularly if it is because they do not have enough security, to apply for a government guarantee for up to 75 per cent of their loan. It replaced the Small Firms Loan Guarantee Scheme.

10. House of Commons Business Innovation and Skills Select Committee inquiry into Government Assistance to Industry (2010)

11. *Risky Business*, Helen Burrows & Kitty Ussher, Demos (2011)

12. Creative Industries Council (CIC) – a joint forum between the creative industries and government, set up to be a voice for creative industries, by focusing on areas where there are barriers to growth facing the sector. More here:

   https://www.gov.uk/government/policy-advisory-groups/ creative-industries-council

   (Accessed 18.08.13)

13. The grant making foundation created by collection society PRS for Music, (Performing Right Society), which administers the music performing rights of composers, songwriters and music publishers.

14. Musicians Benevolent Fund has been renamed to Help Musicians UK since the original publication of this guide.

15. Various interviews, not official ACE figures.

16. Various interviews with PRSF staff.

17. Directory of Social Change, 2010.

18. **http://www.kickstarter.com/help/stats**

19. Interview with Malcolm Dunbar, Pledge Music.

20. **http://bba.org.uk/statistics/article/banks-support-for-smes-quarter-3-2012**

21. **http://www.fsb.org.uk/policy/assets/q3%20vosb%20index.pdf**

22. **http://cdfa.org.uk/about-cdfis/icf/report-archive-inside-community-finance/**

23. **http://isbe.org.uk/content/assets/10.RobertBaldockBP.pdf**

24. Email from Ingenious Ventures, July 2013

25. **http://www.lbangels.co.uk/content/faqs-1**

2. Business Organisation

1. There are two types of company that can use Ltd after their names. A for-profit company, may issue shares and distribute a share of profits to its shareholders, and is described as being a 'company limited by shares'. A not-for-profit company uses its profits for the benefit of members and has no shares, and is described as a 'company limited by guarantee'.

   https://www.gov.uk/browse/business/limited-company

2. Dividends are payments made by companies to their shareholders out of their profits, and are allocated as a fixed amount per share; the larger the percentage of shares the shareholder owns, the greater their total dividends.

3. To form a limited company in the UK you must be registered with Companies House and file an annual return, which gives a snapshot of the company accounts. Details of the requirements can be found here:

    https://www.gov.uk/browse/business/limit-ed-company

    (accessed 31.07.2013) and here:

    http://companieshouse.gov.uk/

    (accessed 31.07.2013)

4. A limited company is sometimes called a 'private' limited company (PLC). A company that offers its shares for sale on the stock exchange is said to have 'gone public' because any member of the public can buy or sell its shares.

5. Gift Aid is a scheme that allows charities to reclaim basic rate tax on donations from UK taxpayers.

6. The Charity Commission www.charitycommission.gov.uk

    in England and Wales.

    The Office of the Scottish Charity Regulator www.oscr.org.uk

    in Scotland.

    Charity Commission for Northern Ireland

    http://www.charitycommissionni.org.uk

    in Northern Ireland.

7. Kickstarter and Indiegogo are US-based crowdfunding sites.

8. Turnover' is defined as the gross amount of money that comes into a company from customers (excluding VAT) and is normally measured over one financial year. The profit is the turnover less the expenses of the company (but before tax is paid).

9. There are insurance products that help businesses manage their risk. Employer's liability insurance is key for any business with employees. Public liability insurance protects you against claims for injury or loss if you interact with members of the public in the course of your business. Professional indemnity insurance can be taken out if you are a professional adviser.

3. Grants

1. Match funding is the requirement of a grant giving body that the recipients raise an equal percentage of the money they require from other sources.

2. A bothy is a small hill-walker's cottage in the highlands of Scotland.

3. *The Seven Laws of Money*, 2nd Edition, Michael Phillips, Shambala (1997)

4. Grant fund schemes have changed since the original publication, but the principles are the same e.g. Grants for the arts were replaced by Project Grants but in principle they are similar as both are small to medium sized grants, funded by

the National Lottery, for time-limited arts projects. Please check funders websites for details of current funds.

5. Music Education Hubs are a network of 123 organisations across England that receive funding administrated by the Arts Council on behalf of Department for Education for facilitating music education in schools.

6. Now called Help Musicians UK aka HMUK and offering a range of creative and welfare support.

4. Friends and Family

1. The loss in year two was in addition to the loss in year one, and not accumulated losses across both years.

2. 2012 UK Membership Survey, Federation of Small Businesses (2012)

5. Crowdfunding

1. BBC Introducing was created in 2007 to support undiscovered musicians via the web platforms, radio shows and live stages that the BBC produces.

2. Pledge Music doesn't exist any longer, having been wound up in 2019 owing money to many artists.

3. Pledge Music allows the option of making a contribution to a charity as part of the campaign.

4. This is a quote from the original interview (29.04.13). For further information see Ward's book written with Oxford-based band Little Fish on being a DIY artist and the nature of success: 'F**k the radio, we've got apple juice', Miranda Ward and Little Fish, Unbound Books (2013)

5. Pledge Music went into administration in 2019 owing money to many artists.

6. Return on Investment.

7. This was confirmed in email correspondence from Indiegogo to the author on 30 July 2013.

6. Sponsorship

1. CSR is the recognition that a company's duties extend beyond its shareholders. For further details and government updates: Corporate Social Responsibility **https://webarchive.nationalarchives.gov.uk/+/http://www.berr.gov. uk/whatwedo/sectors/sustainability/corp-responsibility/ page45192.html**

2. Corporate responsibility: A call for views from the UK Government **https://
   www.gov.uk/government/consultations/corporate-responsibility-
   call-for-views**

7. Debt Finance

1. Project Merlin was the name given to a negotiation between banks and the
   Government in the UK that led to a pledge in February 2011 to lend £190 billion
   in new credit to SMEs **http://www.bankofengland.co.uk/publica-
   tions/Pages/other/monetary/additionaldata.aspx**   [accessed
   31.07.2013].
2. Banking on a Hit, DCMS (2001)
3. Risky Business, Helen Burrows and Kitty Ussher, Demos (2011)
4. Business Bank Strategy Update, Department of Business Innovation and Skills
   (2013)
5. Community Finance For Business 2012 (Community Development Finance
   Association, 2013)
6. Being the Business Bank Strategy Update, Department of Business Innovation
   and Skills (2013)
7. Experian is one of a number of information services companies that allows
   businesses to check credit reports and verify the identity of borrowers.

8. Investment

1. Phonographic Performance Ltd (PPL) administers the collection of recorded
   music royalties for artists, performers and record labels. PRS for Music
   administers the collection of music performance royalties, (commonly referred to
   as PRS).
2. Venture Capital Funding 2nd Edition, Stephen Bloomfield, Kogan Page (2008)
3. A version of the Enterprise Investment Scheme for start-up companies.
4. Business Property Relief provides for ownership in a business to be passed-on, free
   from inheritance tax (relevant if you are investing in a business directly); Sideways
   Loss Relief enables the offsetting of losses from one activity against another profit-
   making activity.
5. Tax relief schemes and the percentages applying to them can vary. These figures
   were correct at the time of publication (August 2013).
6. Confirmed in an email from Patrick Bradley on 1 August 2013.
7. David Glick pointed out that this is a rule of thumb, and that every case is looked
   at on an individual basis.

8. Icebreaker 1 LLP v HMRC. [2010] UKFTT 6 (TC) **http://financeandtaxtribunals.gov.uk/Aspx/view.aspx?id=4687** (accessed 15.08.2013]

9. **http://hmrc.gov.uk/avoidance** spotlight 8 and spotlight 15.

10. **http://ukbusinessangels association.org.uk/**

11. **lbangels.co.uk/**

12. Creative Industries Council Access to Finance Working Group Report, December 2012.

9. Conclusion

1. Investing In Music, IFPI, 2012

2. In *Independence Days, The Story of UK Independent Record Labels*, Alex Ogg, Cherry Red Books (2009) brilliantly documents this period, pointing out that 'Beggars would not have survived without a timely cash injection from WEA', as one of several examples of major label support during the early years of UK Indies.

Acknowledgments

This book is dedicated to my family, particularly Patricia Harris, Roxy 'Arms' Harris and Joseph Caulfield who encouraged me to take up the challenge of writing it, and supported me throughout. Most of all, I have to thank Dr Roxy Harris Snr., without whose support and example it would never have been completed.

I am hugely grateful for guidance given by Jonathan Robinson and Jenny Tyler of MusicTank in wholeheartedly supporting the project from the early stages, and originally publishing the book.

I am so appreciative of all those who agreed to be interviewed, and gave up their valuable time to speak to me, and also those who facilitated introductions, answered daft queries and generally supported the process. I have included below what I hope is a complete list of all those who helped, even if their words were not quoted directly. If I have missed anyone, I sincerely apologise.

List of Interviewees and Correspondents

Amul Batra, Fwinki Music

Berkeley Edwards, Clintons

Brian Message, ATC Management

Bryony Beynon, Creative Sector Services

Ciaran Scullion, Arts Council of Northern Ireland

Danae Ringelmann, Indiegogo

David Glick, Edge Investment

Davin McDermott, CreateTech

Helen Smith, Impala

James Hannam, PRS for Music Foundation

James Yuill

Jim Mawdsley, Generator

Jo Thornton, Generator

Jon Webster, Music Managers Forum

Julia Payne, The Hub

Juliana Koranteng, JayKay Media

Karen Bair, Indiegogo

Kerry Harvey-Piper, Red Grape Music

Kevin Osbourne, MeWe360

Lisa Matthews, Arts Council of Wales

Lisa Morris, Hardwicke and Morris

Malcolm Dunbar, Pledge Music

Martin Goldschmidt, Cooking Vinyl

Mary-Alice Stack, Creative Sector Services

Matt Luxon, Vision Artists

Mike Skeet, Skeet Kaye and Sound Advice

Miranda Ward

Natalie Wade, Small Green Shoots

Natasha Kizzie

Patrick Bradley, Ingenious Media

Penny King, Arts Council England

Phil Nelson, First Column Management

Robert Hicks, Middle of Nowhere Recordings

Ronnie Traynor, Vision Artists

Sam McGregor, Signature Brew

Sofia Hagberg, End of the Road Festival

Stephen Budd, SBM

Stewart Collins, Henley Festival

Tam Coyle, SMIA

Tom Burgess, Pledge Music

Tom Williams, Tom Williams and The Boat

Stuart Thomas, Creative Scotland

Vanessa Reed, PRS for Music Foundation

Wendy Smithers, The Hub

Those Who've Helped

Adam Webb

Alan Davey, Arts Council England

Allan McGowan

Anna Hildur Hildibrandsdottir

Barbara Hillier

Chris Bye, Arts Council England

Chris Cooke, CMU

Doug D'Arcy

Feargal Sharkey

Geoff Travis, Rough Trade

Hamish Harris, Twist Management

Jeremy Silver, Semetric

John Hart

Keith Harris, MusicTank, PPL and Keith Harris Music

Malcolm Buckland

Marianne Frederick, Buzzin' Fly

and Strange Feeling Records Records & Phantasy Sound

Paul Scaife, Record of The Day

Paulette Long

Sam Shemtob, MusicTank and Name PR

Shain Shapiro, Sound Diplomacy

Stephen Hignell, Nordicity

Steve Redmond

Sybil Bell, I Like The Sound Of That

Tamara Gal-On, Capitalise on Creativity

Terri Anderson

Tom Quillfeldt, Name PR

About the Author

Remi Harris is, at heart, someone who loves supporting creative people, and has spent over 20 years finding ways to increase their knowledge and success, whilst being a passionate advocate for diversity in the industry.

A founder staffer at Association of Independent Music in 1999, Remi produced over 100 events, mentoring and training programs, creating the London Connected program while General Manager at

AIM in 2007 to improve access to the digital market for hundreds of indie labels.

As Director of Operations at UK Music in 2011 Remi lobbied for better access to finance for music companies, inspiring her to write the book: Easy Money? The Definitive Guide to Funding Music Projects in the UK (2013) described as *"essential reading for the DIY Sector"*.

Remi chaired the Alliance for Diversity in Music and Media 2007-2012, a group that proposed the first 'diversity pledge' getting diversity on the agenda at industry organisations.

Remi Harris now runs consultancy Remi Harris Consulting where she uses her experiences of working with small businesses and her MBA degree to train and advise creative businesses and people in business skills like planning, fundraising, governance, strategy, freelancing and finance. She was also co-founder of Young Guns Network, the community for young music professionals.

In 2016 she was awarded an MBE for services to the music industry, and in 2019 she was inducted into the UK's Women In Music roll of honour.

www.remiharrisconsulting.com

facebook.com/remiharrisconsulting
twitter.com/remiharrismbe
instagram.com/remiharrismbe
linkedin.com/in/remi-harris-mbe-15220311

Printed in Great Britain
by Amazon

81251080R00133